Gardens To Visit

2005

Publicity Works
P.O. Box 32
Tetbury
Gloucestershire
GL8 8BF

© Tony Russell

Cover picture: Barnsley House

Gardens To Visit 2005

Welcome to *Gardens To Visit 2005* and thank you to the thousands of you who have used *Gardens To Visit 2004* to plan your garden visits during this past year.

It has been tremendously rewarding for all of us involved with the publication to have received so many positive comments and we are delighted that in just three years it has become the main source of information for people who enjoy visiting gardens.

You will be pleased to know that this 2005 edition has increased in content by 30% - so there are now more than 160 of the finest gardens in the UK featured within the publication. Each garden has its own full colour page which includes a beautiful photograph, a 140 word description detailing the main features of the garden and a fact file which provides all the very latest information you need when planning a visit.

Within *Gardens To Visit 2005* there are gardens to suit all tastes, from old favourites such as Sissinghurst, Kew and the Lost Gardens of Heligan, to some very new gardens, such as the exciting 'World Garden' being created at Lullingstone Castle in Kent and The Matara gardens in Gloucestershire.

As you leaf through this book you will see there are gardens to enchant you throughout the year and in every corner of the British Isles extending from north Scotland to the Channel Islands. No matter where you live, this book includes gardens to visit in your locality.

I do hope you enjoy this brand new collection and may I wish you a very successful and enjoyable season of garden outings in 2005.

Tony Russell

Opposite: Borde Hill Garden, Park & Woodland (page 127)

THE GREAT GARDENS COLLECTION
only a few miles apart

Belvoir
Castle

Barnsdale
Gardens

RUTLAND
&
LINCOLNSHIRE

See page 89 - www.belvoircastle.com

See page 113 - www.barnsdalegardens.co.uk

All of these gardens are within easy reach of the A1, located in an undiscovered part of the country.
You need contact only one of us and we will help plan a visit to one or more of the gardens.
See our individual pages in this book or visit any of our websites for further information.
Contact us now to discover more about group rates and special visits.

Grimsthorpe
Castle

Easton Walled
Gardens

See page 93 - www.grimsthorpe.co.uk

See page 92 - www.eastonwalledgardens.co.uk

Contents

Trevarno Estate Gardens & National Museum of Gardening (page 28)

England

"We met at a tea-table, the silver kettle and the conversation reflecting rhododendrons".

Sir Edwin Lutyens

So what is an English garden? Well, as you explore these pages you will begin to see that such is the diversity and individuality of English gardens, that to capture in one sentence the typical English garden is virtually impossible. It is like attempting to capture in a bottle, the sweet mixed fragrance of Philadelphus and rose after the rain has ceased on a warm June evening.

Be it the garden or the fragrance, enjoy them as you can and commit their charm to memory.

Opposite: Holker Hall and Gardens (page 34)

The Swiss Garden was created in the early nineteenth century. It contains picturesque features hidden in an undulating nine-acre landscape. The garden is planted with magnificent trees and ornamental shrubs which are arranged in a series of glades, lawns and winding walks, designed to provide unexpected vistas. The recently refurbished and replanted, subterranean grotto and fernery nestles in the centre. 'The Grand Tour' provided inspiration for the tiny thatched Swiss Cottage. The fashion for 'Swiss" architecture, so popular in the Regency period can be seen all around the Garden. Elegant floral arches and a network of ponds with decorative bridges and delightful islands complete the picture. Peafowl roam freely in the garden. Spring bulbs, rhododendrons and rambling roses are spectacular in season. Benches are located at frequent intervals. There is also an adjacent picnic area and a woodland lakeside walk.

Fact File

Opening Times:	November 1st to March 31st 10am - 4pm, April 1st to October 31st 10am - 5pm
Admission Rates:	Adults £4.00, Senior Citizen £3.00, Child Free.
Group Rates:	Miimum group size: 20 but all groups welcome
	Adults £3.00, Senior Citizen £2.00, Child Free.
Facilities:	Visitor Centre, Restaurant, Toilets, Gift/Souvenirs and Plant Stall.
Disabled Access:	Yes, Toilet and parking for disabled on site. Wheelchairs on loan, booking advised.
Tours/Events:	Guided Tours and Group Bookings by appointment.
Coach Parking:	Yes.
Length of Visit:	2 hours
Booking Contact:	Karen Wilsher
	The Swiss Garden, Old Warden Park, Old Warden, Biggleswade, Bedfordshire, SG18 9ER.
	Telephone: 01767 626228 Fax: 01767 627053
Email:	kwilsher@shuttleworth.org
Website:	www.shuttleworth.org
Location:	Approximately 2 miles west of Biggleswade A1 roundabout signposted from A1 and A600.

Please quote this guide when booking

Savill Garden - Windsor Great Park   Surrey

World renowned 35 acre woodland garden within Windsor Great Park which was created in 1932 by Sir Eric Savill from an undeveloped area of the Park. Spectacular Spring displays: formal rose gardens and herbaceous borders in Summer; fiery colours of Autumn and misty vistas of Winter. The unique temperate house shelters frost-tender plants from the rigours of Winter - 'a piece of woodland under glass'.

In celebration of the Golden Jubilee, a new area has been created, designed by award winning Barbara Hunt; planting created and executed by Lyn Randall, Head of the Savill Garden, and a water sculpture by Barry Mason. The theme is soft and peaceful, a summer garden with hard landscaping.

Having walked round this delightful garden, enjoy a relaxing meal in the excellent restaurant and perhaps treat yourself to something from the plant and gift shop, An oasis of tranquillity 5 miles from Windsor.

Fact File

Opening Times: 10am - 6pm March - October, 10am - 4pm November - February.
Admission Rates: Seasonal - Adults £3.50 - £5.50, Senior Citizen £3.00 - £5.00, Child £1.25 - £2.50
Group Rates: Minimum group size: 10
Seasonal - Adults £3.00 - £5.00, Senior Citizen £3.00 - £5.00, Child £1.25 - £2.50
Facilities: Shop, Plant Sales, Teas, Restaurant.
Disabled Access: Yes. Toilet and Parking for disabled on site. Wheelchairs on loan.
Tours/Events: Guided tours for groups, bookable in advance.
On-going programme of events - please contact for details.
Coach Parking: Yes.
Length of Visit: 3 - 4 hours
Booking Contact: Julie Hill
Crown Estate Office, The Great Park, Windsor, Berkshire, SL4 2HT
Telephone: 01753 847518 Fax: 01753 847536
Email: savillgarden@thecrownestate.co.uk
Website: www.savillgarden.co.uk
Location: Clearly signposted from Ascot, Bagshot, Egham, Windsor, Old Windsor and A30.

Please quote this guide when booking

A woodland garden on the grand scale; set beneath the canopies of beautiful mature trees with delightful views to Virginia Water Lake. Over 200 acres of camellias rhododendrons, magnolias and many other flowering trees and shrubs provide visitors with breathtaking displays in March, April and May.

Massed plantings of hydrangeas are the highlight of the summer before a myriad of autumn tints from Japanese maples, birches, sweet gums and tupelos light up the woods.

Winter brings the flowers of witch-hazel and drifts of heathers amongst the dwarf conifers in the Heather Garden before swathes of dwarf daffodils stud the turf in the sweeping Azalea Valley.

Truly a garden for all seasons.

Fact File

Opening Times: Car park open: 8am - 7pm (4pm in winter) or sunset if earlier.
Admission Rates: Car Park Charges only: April & May £5.50, June - March £4.00
Facilities: At nearby Savill Garden.
Disabled Access: Yes, but limited. Toilet and parking for disabled on site.
Tours/Events: None.
Coach Parking: No. Coaches by arrangement on weekdays only.
Length of Visit: 2 - 3 hours
Booking Contact: Julie Hill
Valley Gardens - The Great Park, Windsor, Berkshire, SL4 2HT
Telephone: 01753 847518 Fax: 01753 847536
Email: savillgarden@thecrownestate.co.uk
Website: None
Location: On the eastern boundary of Windsor Great Park (off A30)
Access to Valley Gardens car park via Wick Road.

Please quote this guide when booking

Waltham Place Organic Farm & Garden — Berkshire

With a history dating back for a thousand years, Waltham Place has entered a new era. Within the formal layout of mellow brick walls, some dating back to the 17th Century, lie ornamental gardens planted in the new naturalistic style with seeping curves of gravel and billowing grasses.

Ancient pergolas support a riot of roses. Within these 40 acres of garden are also to be found a butterfly garden, a herb garden and a Japanese garden. The undulating long borders protecting beech alcoves lead down to the lake and the woodland beyond. One of the finest specimens of weeping beech in the U.K. is to be found her at Waltham. These and more are part of the 170 acres Organic farm and estate and are complemented by the organic farm shop and tearoom.

Fact File

Opening Times: June to September; Wednesday & Fridays 10am - 4pm (Wednesday for NGS, Fridays by appointment only).

Admission Rates: Adults £3.50, Senior Citizen £3.50, Child £1.00

Facilities: Organic Farm Shop, Tea Room, Plant Sales, Education Centre.

Disabled Access: Yes. Toilet and parking for disabled on site.

Tours/Events: Monthly seasonal walks, group tours by arrangement.

Coach Parking: Not on site but very close by.

Length of Visit: 2 hours

Booking Contact: Estate Office
Waltham Place, Church Hill, White Waltham, Berks SL6 3JH
Telephone: 01628 825517 Fax: 01628 825045

Email: estateoffice@walthamplace.com

Website: www.walthamplace.com

Location: From M4 junction 8/9 take A404M and follow signs to White Waltham. Turn left to Windsor and Paley Street. Farm on left handside.

Please quote this guide when booking

With its ornamental lakes, monuments and temples nestling amidst glorious open spaces and wooded valleys, Stowe Landscape Gardens is one of the supreme creations of the Georgian era.

Described as a 'work to wonder at', the gardens explore ideas about love, liberty, virtue and politics and have been inspiring writers, artists and visitors for over three centuries. Today the splendour and magic of Stowe can be enjoyed by all.

The gardens were given to the National Trust in 1990, and an ambitious programme of restoration is underway to recapture their former unparalleled magnificence.

Whether you want to walk in enchanting surroundings, a chance to step back in time, or an unspoilt setting for a family picnic. Stowe is the perfect place for a day out. National Trust shop, tea room, guided tours and a full programme of fun events for all the family.

Fact File

Opening Times: 28th Feb - 31 Oct 10am - 5.30pm Wednesday to Sunday. 1 Nov - 27th Feb 10am - 4pm Saturday and Sunday. (Closed Dec 24th/25th).

Admission Rates: Adults £5.80, Senior Citizen £5.80, Child £2.90, Family £14.50.

Group Rates: Pre-booked groups of 15 or more £4.90.

Facilities: National Trust Shop, Tea Room and Kiosk. Audio Visual Show.

Disabled Access: Yes. Toilet and Parking for disabled on site. Self powered vehicle for loan booking necessary.

Tours/Events: Guided tours available.

Coach Parking: Yes

Length of Visit: Approx 2 hours - All day.

Booking Contact: Visitor Reception - 01280 818825
Stowe Landscape Gardens, Buckingham, MK18 5EH.
Telephone: 01280 822850

Email: stowegarden@nationaltrust.org.uk

Website: www.nationaltrust.org.uk/stowegardens

Location: 3 miles NW of Buckingham via Stowe Avenue off A422 Buckingham - Banbury Road
Oxford 18 miles/Northampton/ Milton Keynes 14 Miles.

Please quote this guide when booking

Waddesdon Manor   Buckinghamshire

Waddesdon Manor and Grounds were bequeathed to the National Trust by the Rothschilds in 1957. The garden today is essentially the one laid out by Baron Ferdinand de Rothschild and his French landscape designer, Elie Laine in the 19th century. It is one of the finest Victorian gardens in Britain, with a parterre, colourful shrubs, rose garden and specimen trees.

The gardens can be enjoyed at any season with its seasonal displays, walks, fountains and statuary. At its heart is the Aviary stocked with exotic birds and known for breeding endangered species.

Fact File

Opening Times:	Grounds - Weekends in Jan, Feb & Mar (from Jan 8th). 23rd March - 23rd December (Wed to Sun, Bank Hol Mondays and Mon 19th and Tues 20th December) 10am - 5pm.
Admission Rates:	Adults £4.00, Child £2.00, National Trust Members free.
Group Rates:	Minimum group size: 15
	Adults £3.20, Child £1.60, National Trust Members free.
Facilities:	Gift & Wine Shops, Plant Sales, Manor & Stables Restaurants.
Disabled Access:	Yes. Toilet and parking for disabled on site. Wheelchairs on loan.
Tours/Events:	Contact the booking office for details.
Coach Parking:	Yes.
Length of Visit:	Minimum 2 hours.
Booking Contact:	Stephanie Wyatt
	Waddesdon, Nr Aylesbury, Buckinghamshire, HP18 0JH
	Tel: 01296 653226 Fax: 01296 653212
Email:	stephanie.wyatt@nationaltrust.org.uk
Website:	www.waddesdon.org.uk
Location:	On the A41 between Aylesbury & Bicester.

Please quote this guide when booking

Elgood's Brewery Gardens   Cambridgeshire

A beautiful 4-acre garden, situated behind Elgood's Brewery, on the banks of the River Nene in Wisbech, in the heart of the Fens.

The garden is famous for its maze and its trees, some over 150 years old, including Ginkgo Biloba, Tulip Tree, and Tree of Heaven. There is a lake with golden and ghost carp, a pond, which is home to Great Crested Newts, and a hot-house with lemons, orchids, and other tropical plants.

The Visitor Centre houses a museum with brewery artefacts and pub memorabilia. A variety of freshly prepared snacks are available in the licensed cafe-bar and there is a well-stocked shop selling quality beers, gifts and plants.

Close by are The Octavia Hill Museum, The Wisbech & Fenland Museum, and the National Trust's Peckover House. These attractions, together with several excellent pubs along the riverbanks, add up to an interesting and unusual visit.

Fact File

Opening Times:	26th April - 29th September 2005 11.30am - 4.30pm.
Admission Rates:	Garden & Brewery - Adults £6.00, Senior Citizens £6.00, Child £4.00
	Garden only - Adults £2.50, Senior Citizen £2.00, Child £2.00
Groups Rates:	Minimum group size Daytime 10, Evening 20
	Garden & Brewery - £5.00, Garden Only - £2.00
Facilities:	Visitor Centre, Gift Shop, Plant Sales, Teas, Licensed bar.
Disabled Access:	Yes. Toilets and parking for disabled on site. Wheelchairs on loan. Booking Advisable.
Tours/Events:	Brewery Tours Tues, Wed, and Thurs 2pm (not suitable for disabled)
Coach Parking:	Yes
Length of Visit:	1 - 2+ Hours
Booking Contact:	Kate Pateman
	North Brink, Wisbech, Cambridge, PE13 1LN
	Telephone: 01945 583160 Fax: 01945 587711
Email:	elgoods-brewery.co.uk
Website:	www.elgoods-brewery.co.uk
Location:	Wisbech

Please quote this guide when booking

The Manor, Hemingford Grey   Cambridgeshire

A Storybook garden for children of any age - but there is much more than a garden here, for the wonderful moated Norman Manor, c.1130, is one of the three oldest continuously inhabited houses in England. It was the home of Lucy Boston from 1939 and the setting for her Green Knowe children's books. She started the garden by planting yew bushes and for the Queen's Coronation cut them into crowns and orbs, later creating chess pieces which now stand in black and white squares. She filled long parallel borders with old-fashioned roses and scented perennials. To begin with, Graham Stuart Thomas advised Lucy on the choice of roses and bearded irises (many of the latter are Dykes Medal winners). At the Norman front are ancient yews and a superb copper beech that has layered itself. Parts of the garden are left wild deliberately.

Fact File

Opening Times: Daily, All Year, 11am - 5pm (4pm in Winter)
Admission Rates: Adults £2.00, Senior Citizen £2.00, Child Free.
Facilities: Gift Shop, Plant Sales.
Disabled Access: Partial. Toilet (for emergency use only) and parking (2 cars at house only) for disabled on site.
Tours/Events: None
Coach Parking: No, but nearby
Length of Visit: 1 + hours
Booking Contact: Mrs Diana Boston
                       The Manor, Hemingford Grey, Huntingdon, Cambridgeshire, PE28 9BN
                       Telephone: 01480 463134 Fax: 01480 465026
Email: diana_boston@hotmail.com
Website: www.greenknowe.co.uk
Location: By Car - Hemingford Grey is 4 miles south-east of Huntingdon, just off the A14.
                       By Train - To Huntingdon on Kings Cross line and then Bus or Taxi.
                       By Bus - No 5 Cambridge - Huntingdon, Bus stops in Hemingford Grey.

Please quote this guide when booking

Set in the heart of the Cheshire countryside, Adlington Hall has been the home of the Legh family since 1315. The Hall itself, a magnificent English country house, incorporates Tudor, Elizabethan and Georgian architecture and houses a 17th century organ played by Handel.

The 2,000 acre Estate, landscaped in the 18th century, contains beautiful gardens in the style of 'Capability' Brown complete with a ha-ha. The ancient Lime Avenue, dating from 1688, leads to a woodland 'Wilderness' with winding paths, temples, bridges and follies. A path through the Laburnum Arcade leads into the formal Rose Garden, then on to the Maze created in English Yew. The Father Tiber Water Garden provides a peaceful haven with its ponds, fountains and water cascade and the newly created Penstemon Garden provides a colourful addition to the East Wing. Other features include a large herbaceous border, rockeries, specimen trees, azaleas and rhododendrons.

Fact File

Opening Times:	June, July, August: Wednesday only 2pm - 5pm.
	Open weekdays throughout the year for groups by prior arrangement.
Admission Rates:	Adults £5.00, Senior Citizens £5.00, Child £2.00.
Groups Rates:	Minimum group size: 20
	Adults £4.00, Senior Citizens £4.00, Child £2.00.
Facilities:	Tea Room.
Disabled Access:	Limited. Toilet and parking for disabled on site.
Tours/Events:	Guided tours by appointment. Please telephone for details of special events.
Coach Parking:	Yes
Length of Visit:	3 hours
Booking Contact:	The Guide
	Adlington Hall, Adlington. Macclesfield, Cheshire, SK10 4LF
	Telephone: 01625 820875 Fax: 01625 828756
Email:	enquiries@adlingtonhall.com
Website:	www. adlingtonhall.com
Location:	5 miles north of Macclesfield off A523 turn left at Adlington crossroads onto Mill Lane.
	Entrance 1/2 mile on left.

Please quote this guide when booking

Cholmondeley Castle Garden   Cheshire

Cholmondeley Castle Garden is said by many to be among the most romantically beautiful gardens they have seen. Even the wild orchids, daisies and buttercups take on an aura of glamour in this beautifully landscaped setting. Visitors enter by the deer park mere - one of two strips of water which are home to many types of waterfowl and freshwater fish. Those who take advantage of the picnic site can walk round the lake and enjoy the splendid view of the Gothic Castle which stands so dramatically on the hill surrounded by sweeping lawns and magnificent trees; two enormous cedars of lebanon and great spreading oaks among sweet chestnut, lime, beech and plane. Whatever the season there is always a wealth of plants and shrubs in flower from the earliest bulbs through many varieties of magnolia, camellia, azalea and rhododendrons. Followed by a golden canopied laburnum grove, a very fine *davidia involucrata* in the glade, and varieties of cornus. There is also a very pretty rose garden surrounded by mixed borders, containing a large variety of herbaceous plants and shrubs.

Fact File

Opening Times: April to September. (Castle not open to public).
Wednesday, Thursday, Sunday (Bank Holidays and Good Friday).
Admission Rates: Adults £4.00, Child £1.50.
Group Rates: Minimum group size: 25
Facilities: Shop, Plant Sales, Teas.
Disabled Access: Yes. Toilet and parking for disabled on site,
Tours/Events: Please ring to enquire about special events, plant fares, plays, concerts.
Coach Parking: Yes
Length of Visit: 3 - 4 hours
Booking Contact: Cholmondeley Castle, Malpas, Cheshire, SY14 8AH
Telephone: 01829 720383 Fax: 01829 720877
Email: pennypritchard@supanet.com
Website: None.
Location: 7 miles west of Nantwich, 6 miles north of Whitchurch on A49.

Please quote this guide when booking

Approximately 100 acres of Woodland Gardens and natural woodland bordering the Lynher Estuary featuring extensive woodlands and riverside walks.

The garden contains the national collection of *Camellia japonica*. There are a wide variety of camellias, magnolias, rhododendrons and other flowering trees and shrubs, numerous wild flowers and birds in beautiful surrounds.

Fact File

Opening Times:	11am to 5.30pm, everyday excluding Mondays and Fridays. Open Bank holiday Monday and Good Friday. 1st March to 31st October.
Admission Rates:	Adults £4.00, Senior Citizen £4.00, Child under 16 free.
Group Rates:	As admission rates.
Facilities:	Teas, Restaurant, shop (Available only on Antony House open days).
Disabled Access:	Yes over rough terrain in parts. Parking for disabled on site.
Tours/Events:	Tours available for parties on request.
Coach Parking:	Yes
Length of Visit:	between 1 - 2 hours
Booking Contact:	Mrs V Anderson Antony, Torpoint, Cornwall, PL11 2QA Telephone: 01752 812364
Email:	paul.cressy@colvilles.co.uk
Website:	None
Location:	From the A38 Trerulefoot roundabout follow brown tourist signs for Antony House. At Antony House continue past the house down the drive. The Woodland Gardens can be found on the left hand side.

Please quote this guide when booking

Lush, unmanicured and utterly magical, Carwinion Garden lies in a sheltered Cornish valley on the Helford River. Ponds, waterfalls and sheltered pathways are dotted amongst the towering trees, bamboos and well-established plants in this twelve acre family run garden.

The garden contains a plethora of specimen plants, immense tree ferns over a hundred years old, gunnera with leaves spanning over two metres and ferns and Hellebores which flourish in the dappled sunlit woodland. Carwinion has one of the largest collections of bamboos in England; over a hundred and sixty different varieties can be found growing throughout the garden.

The garden is at its pinnacle in Spring-time when the impact of colour, the bluebell carpeted woodland, the fragrance of the Azaleas and the continued blooming of the Camellias provides a sensual experience not to be missed.

Fact File

Opening Times: All Year, every day 10am - 5.30pm
Admission Rates: Adults £3.50, Senior Citizens £3.50, Child Free (under 16).
Group Rates: Minimum group size: 10
Adults £3.00, Senior Citizens £3.00.
Facilities: Plant Sales, Teas (2 - 5.30pm from May - Sept), Small Gift Shop.
Disabled Access: Partial. Toilet and parking for disabled on site.
Tours/Events: Occasional Art Exhibits displayed in Gardens and House. Theatre and Annual fairy trail for children.
Coach Parking: Yes, by arrangement
Length of Visit: 1 - 2 hours
Booking Contact: Peverell Rogers
Carwinion, Carwinion Road, Mawnan Smith, Nr Falmouth, Cornwall, TR11 5JA
Telephone: 01326 250258 Fax: 01326 250903
Email: pev@carwinion.co.uk
Website: www.carwinion.co.uk
Location: Five miles South-West of Falmouth, in the village of Mawnan Smith, North side of the Helford River.

Please quote this guide when booking

Cotehele, owned by the Edgecumbe family for nearly 600 years, is a fascinating and enchanting estate set on the steep wooded slopes of the River Tamar. Exploring Cotehele's many and various charms provides a full day out for the family and leaves everyone longing to return.

A walk through the garden and along the river leads to the quay where the restored Tamar sailing barge *Shamrock* is moored. Cotehele Mill is to be found tucked away in the woods. Restored to working order and now grinding corn to produce flour, (which can be purchased) the 0.3mile walk from the Quay is a must.

Fact File

Opening Times:	All Year.
Admission Rates:	Adults £4.40, Child £2.20.
Group Rates:	Minimum group size: 15 +
Facilities:	Shop, Plant Sales, Teas and Restaurant.
Disabled Access:	Partial. Toilet and parking for disabled on site. Wheelchairs on loan.
Tours/Events:	None
Coach Parking:	Yes
Length of Visit:	3 hours
Booking Contact:	Leesa Clements
	Cotehele, St Dominick, Saltash, Cornwall. PL12 6TA
	Telephone: 01579 351346 Fax: 01579 351222
Email:	cotehele@nationaltrust.org.uk
Website:	www.nationaltrust.org.uk
Location:	On the west (Cornish) bank of the Tamar, 8 miles SW of Tavistock, 14 miles east of St Dominick.

Please quote this guide when booking

Heligan, seat of the Tremayne family for more than 400 years, is one of the most mysterious estates in England. At the end of the nineteenth century its thousand acres were at their zenith, but only a few years after the Great War of 1914 bramble and ivy were already drawing a green veil over this sleeping beauty.

After decades of neglect, the devastating hurricane of 1990 should have consigned the Lost Gardens of Heligan to a footnote in history. Instead, fired by a magnificent obsession to bring these once glorious gardens back to life, a small band of enthusiasts has grown into a large working team with its own vision for Heligan's future.

Today "The Nation's Favourite Garden" offers 200 acres for exploration, which include extensive productive gardens and pleasure grounds, subtropical jungle, sustainably-managed farmland, wetlands and ancient woodlands, and a pioneering wildlife conservation project.

Fact File

Opening Times: All year.

Admission Rates: Adults £7.50, Senior Citizens £7.00, Child £4.00

Groups Rates: Minimum group size 20, prior booking is essential.
Adults £7.00, Senior Citizens £6.50, Child £4.00

Facilities: Licensed Restaurant, Tea Rooms, Lunchtime Servery, Bar, Heligan Shop and Plant Sales, Lobbs Farm Shop.

Disabled Access: Yes. Toilets and parking for disabled on site. Wheelchairs on loan.

Tours/Events: Please telephone for seasonal details.

Coach Parking: Yes

Length of Visit: At least 4 hours

Booking Contact: Group Bookings Department.
The Lost Gardens of Heligan Pentewan, St Austell, Cornwall, PL26 6EN.
Telephone: 01726 845120   Fax: 01726 845121

Email: groups@heligan.com

Website: www.heligan.com

Location: From St Austell, take the Mevagissey Road (B3273) and follow the brown tourist signs to "The Lost Gardens of Heligan".

Please quote this guide when booking

One of only three Grade 1 listed Cornish Gardens set within the 865 acres of the Country Park overlooking the Plymouth Sound. Sir Richard Edgcumbe of Cotehele built a new home in his deer park at Mount Edgcumbe in 1547. Miraculously the walls of this red stone Tudor House survived a direct hit by bombs in 1941 and it was restored by the 6th Earl in 1958. It is now beautifully furnished with family possessions.

The two acre Earl's Garden was created beside the House in the 18th century. Ancient and rare trees including a 400 year old lime, a splendid Lucombe oak and a Mexican pine, are set amidst classical garden houses and an exotic Shell Seat. Colourful flowers and heather grace the re-created Victorian East Lawn terrace. Also formal 18th Century Gardens in Italian, French & English style, modern American and New Zealand sections. There are over 1000 varieties in the National Camellia Collection which received the international award of 'Camellia Garden of Excellence'.

Fact File

Opening Times:	House & Earls Garden open 27th March - 29th September, Sunday to Thursday 11am - 4.30pm; Country Park open all year.
Admission Rates:	Adults £4.50, Senior Citizen £3.50, Child £2.25
Groups Rates:	Minimum group size: 10 (March - October) Adults £3.50, Senior Citizen £3.50, Child £2.00
Facilities:	Shop & Tea Room in House. Orangery Restaurant (limited opening in winter), Civil Weddings, Conference Facilities.
Disabled Access:	Yes. Toilet and parking for disabled on site. Wheelchairs on loan, booking necessary.
Tours/Events:	Guided tours of the gardens available all year. Historic buildings, Camellia Collection in season. Exhibition and events programme.
Coach Parking:	Yes
Length of Visit:	2 hours
Booking Contact:	Secretary. Mount Edgcumbe House, Cremyll, Torpoint, Cornwall, PL10 1HZ Telephone : 01752 822236 Fax: 01752 822199
Email:	mt.edgcumbe@plymouth.gov.uk
Website:	www.mountedgcumbe.gov.uk
Location:	FromPlymouth Cremyll Foot Ferry, Torpoint Ferry or Saltash Bridge. From Cornwall via Liskeard - to A374, B3247, follow brown signs.

Please quote this guide when booking

Pencarrow, a Georgian house with 50 acres of Grade 2* listed Gardens, must be one of Cornwall's finest stately homes. It is still privately owned and lived in by the Molesworth-St Aubyn's, who purchased the estate in the reign of Queen Elizabeth I. Pencarrow lies at the foot of a valley midway between Bodmin and Wadebridge. It is approached through a mile long drive flanked by well planned woodland, nearly 700 varieties of rhododendrons, camellias and hydrangeas.

The imposing Palladian style house built in 1771, contains a superb collection of paintings by many famous artists, including a unique collection of works by Sir Joshua Reynolds, set amongst outstanding furniture and porcelain. In 1882 during his visit Sir Arthur Sullivan composed much of the music for his comic opera 'Iolanthe'. Pencarrow was the National Heritage Award winner in 1997, 98 and 99 (also voted by its visitors "Best Historic House in the United Kingdom"). In 2004 it received The Dogs' Trust national award as Dogs' Tourist attraction of the year.

Fact File

Opening Times: The house is open Sun to Thurs 27th March to 27th October, 11am-5pm (last tour 4pm). The Gardens are open 7 days a week 1st March to 31st October 9.30am - 5.30pm.

Admission Rates: House & Gardens: Adults £7.50, Child £3.50. Gardens only: Adults £4.00, Child £1.00

Groups Rates: Minimum group size: 20 - 30, Adults £6.50, Child £3.25 31 + Adults £5.50, Child £2.25

Facilities: House, Shop, Craft Gallery, Plant Sales, Children's Play Area, Tea Rooms serving light lunches and cream teas.

Disabled Access: Yes. Toilet and parking for disabled on site.

Tours/Events: Guided tours around the house (last tour 4pm) - Garden tours for group bookings. Jazz in Gardens, Theatre, Concerts, Conference Room, Wedding License.

Coach Parking: Yes.

Length of Visit: 2 1/2 - 5 hours

Booking Contact: James Reynolds. Pencarrow, Washaway, Bodmin, Cornwall, PL30 3AG. Telephone: 01208 841369   Fax: 01208 841722

Email: pencarrow@aol.com

Website: www.pencarrow.co.uk

Location: Four miles north west of Bodmin, signed off the A389 and B3266 at Washaway.

Please quote this guide when booking

Pine Lodge Gardens & Nursery   Cornwall

The 30- acre estate comprises gardens within a garden which hold a wide range of some 6000 plants, all of which are labelled. In addition to rhododendrons, magnolias and camellias so familiar in Cornish gardens here are Mediterranean and southern-hemisphere plants grown for all year round interest. Herbaceous borders, a fernery, a formal garden, a woodland walk, shrubberies and a wild flower meadow.

The water features include a large wildlife pond, an ornamental pond with cascades (stocked with koi carp), a lake with an island (home for black swans and water fowl) and marsh gardens. Trees are also a speciality with an acer glade, a collection of 80 conifers, all different, in a four acre Pinetum, an Arboretum and an acre Japanese garden. Holder of the National collection of Grevilleas. Seeds brought back on Seed Hunting Exhibitions every year for our Nursery of Rare & Unusual Plants. The gardens were given a Highly Commended Award by the Cornish Tourist Board for 2002.

Fact File

Opening Times:	1st March - 31st October. Nursery open all year.
Admission Rates:	Adults £5.00, Child £3.00.
Groups Rates:	Minimum group size: 20 - Adults £4.50
Facilities:	Plant Sales, Tea Room, Shop.
Disabled Access:	Partial. Toilet and parking for disabled on site, Wheelchairs on loan, booking necessary.
Tours/Events:	Tours everyday, booking essential. Wood Turning demonstration everyday.
Coach Parking:	Yes.
Length of Visit:	3 hours
Booking Contact:	Shirley Clemo. Pine Lodge Gardens, Holmbush, St Austell, Cornwall, PL25 3RQ Telephone: 01726 73500 Fax: 01726 77370
Email:	garden@pine-lodge.co.uk
Website:	www.pine-lodge.co.uk
Location:	Situated on the A390 2 miles east of St Austell

Please quote this guide when booking

Steeply wooded 25 acre sub-tropical ravine garden falls 200 feet from 18th century house to private beach on Helford River.

A stream cascades over waterfalls through ponds full of Koi Carp and exotic water plants, winds through 2 acres of blue and white hydrangeas and spills out over the beach. Huge Australian tree ferns and palms mingle with shrubs of ever changing colours and scent beneath over-arching canopy of 100 year old rhododendrons and magnolias. A giant plantation of gunnera and clumps of huge bamboos give the garden a unique and exotic wildness matches by no other garden in the British Isles.

The newly build Hibbert Centre houses a distinctive restaurant, garden and gift shop. Children love Trebah, as do dogs (welcome on leads).

Fact File

Opening Times: Open every day of the year 10.30am to 5pm.

Admission Rates: Adults £5.50, Senior Citizen £5.00, Child £3.00.

Group Rates: Minimum group size: 12
Adults £4.00, Senior Citizen £4.00, Child £2.00.

Facilities: Visitor Centre, Shop, Plant Sales, Teas, Restaurant.

Disabled Access: Yes, Toilet and parking for disabled on site. Wheelchairs on loan, booking advised.

Tours/Events: Free welcome talk on arrival, full guided tour of one and a half hours at an extra £1 per head - must be booked in advance.

Coach Parking: Yes.

Length of Visit: 2 1/2 - 3 hours

Booking Contact: V Woodcroft
Trebah Garden, Mawnan Smith, Falmouth, Cornwall, TR11 5JZ.
Telephone: 01326 250448 Fax: 01326 250781

Email: mail@trebah-garden.co.uk

Website: www.trebah-garden.co.uk

Location: From north - A39 from Truro to Treliever Cross Roundabout, follow brown and white tourism signs to Trebah.

Please quote this guide when booking

Tregrehan

The garden at Tregrehan is a large planted woodland area surrounding a more formal walled garden complete with a fine original glasshouse range. It is listed by English Heritage as outstanding.

A guided tour usually takes two hours, giving time for light refreshments at the conclusion. There is also a small nursery selling plants propagated from the garden. The appeal of visiting Tregrehan lies in the non-commercial approach of the owners and the diversity of the plants grown.

The backbone of the garden is the planting of exotica from the early 19th century onwards, many of which have reached exceptional size for the UK. To complement this Victorian passion for new plants William Nesfield redesigned in 1845 the more formal areas around the house.

Much planting is still undertaken from known natural sources creating a future Green Gene Bank, within a Temperate Cornish Rainforest!

Fact File

Opening Times:	Mid March - Mid June, Wednesday - Sunday incl. Bank Holiday Mondays (Closed Easter Sunday) 10.30 - 17.00. Also Mid June - End August, Wed 14.00 - 17.00.
Admission Rates:	Adults £4.00, Senior Citizens £4.00, Child Free
Groups Rates:	Minimum group size 10
Facilities:	Plant Sales, Teas
Disabled Access:	Partial (1/2 Garden). Toilet and parking for disabled on site.
Tours/Events:	Guided tours included for groups over 10, by appointment anytime.
Coach Parking:	Yes
Length of Visit:	2 Hours
Booking Contact:	T Hudson
	Tregrehan House, Par, Cornwall. PL24 2SJ
	Telephone: 01726 814389 Fax: 01726 814389
Email:	None
Website:	None
Location:	On A390 2 miles east of St Austell 1/2 mile west of St Blazey.

Please quote this guide when booking

Trevarno Estate & National Museum of Gardening   Cornwall

A unique and unforgettable gardening experience comprising sixty acres of beautiful Victorian and Georgian Gardens and Ground, the amazing National Museum of Gardening and a range of fascinating craft workshops and display areas inspired by the estate and gardens. Trevarno is a jewel in the Cornish crown having one of the countries largest and most diverse plant collections, many contrasting features, abundant wildlife and a major restoration project within two walled gardens. After exploring the tranquil woodland walks, lakeside terraces, mysterious rockery and grotto, and more formal areas including the Sunken Italian Garden and Serpentine Yew Tunnel, relax and enjoy homemade refreshments amongst the sub-tropical plants in the delightful Fountain Garden Conservatory. But leave plenty of time to see the unique National Museum of Gardening, a fascinating celebration of Britain's glorious gardening heritage. Don't forget the famous Handmade Soap Workshop and Organic Herbal Workshop, Soap Collection and Toy Museum.

Fact File

Opening Times:	10.30am - 5pm all year.
Admission Rates:	Adults £4.95, Senior Citizens £4.25, Child £1.95, Disabled £2.75.
Group Rates:	Minimum group size: 12
	Adults £4.25, Senior Citizen £3.75, Child £1.25.
Facilities:	The National Museum of Gardening, Shop, Plant Sales, Teas, Craft Workshops, Soap Collection, *Vintage Toy Collection (*small additional charge).
Disabled Access:	Partial. Toilet and parking for disabled on site. Wheelchairs on loan, booking essential.
Tours/Events:	Numerous events throughout the year. Please call for details.
Coach Parking:	Yes, for up to 6 coaches.
Length of Visit:	4 hours
Booking Contact:	Garden Co-ordinator
	Trevarno Estate, Trevarno Manor, Crowntown, Nr Helston, Cornwall, TR13 ORU
	Telephone: 01326 574274 Fax: 01326 574282
Email:	enquiry@trevarno-fsnet.co.uk
Website:	Under construction
Location:	Trevarno is located immediately east of Crowntown village - leave Helston on Penzance Road and follow the brown signs.

Please quote this guide when booking

Trewithen Gardens Cornwall

Trewithen means 'house of the trees' and the name truly describes this fine early Georgian house in its splendid setting of wood and parkland.

Country Life described the house as 'one of the outstanding West Country houses of the 18th century' and Penelope Hobhouse has described the garden as 'perhaps the most beautiful woodland garden in England'.

2004 was the 100th year in which George Johnstone inherited Trewithen and started developing the gardens as we know them today. The great glade on the south side is a masterpiece of landscape gardening and is a monument to the genius of George Johnstone. These gardens covering some thirty acres are renowned for their magnificent collection of camellias, rhododendrons, magnolias and many rare trees and shrubs which are seldom found elsewhere in Britain. The extensive woodland gardens are surrounded by traditional landscaped parkland.

Fact File

Opening Times:	Open 1st February to 30th September, 10am to 4.30pm Monday to Saturday. Sundays (March, April and May only).
Admission Rates:	Adults £4.75 March to June, £4.25 July to September.
Groups Rate:	Minimum group size: 20 Group £4.25 March to June, £4.00 July to September.
Facilities:	Trewithen Tea Shop, Plant Sales, Camera Obscura, Viewing Platforms.
Disabled Access:	Yes. Toilet and Parking for disabled on site. Wheelchairs on loan.
Tours/Events:	Guided tours available, prior booking is essential. Occasional special events please telephone for details.
Coach Parking:	Yes
Length of Visit:	2 - 2 1/2 hours
Booking Contact:	Glenys Cates Trewithen Gardens, Grampound Road, Nr Truro, Cornwall, TR2 4DD Telephone: 01726 883647 Fax: 01726 882301
Email:	gardens@trewithen-estate.demon.co.uk
Website:	www.trewithengardens.co.uk
Location:	On the A390 between Truro and St Austell.

Please quote this guide when booking

Cumbria - The Lake District

I often tell people I've got the best rockery and the best hard landscaping in Britain in my back garden. They are called the Wastwater Screes and Great Gable and Scafell.

The mists and mountains and shifting lights of Lakeland have long been an inspiration to garden designers. So many of the Cumbrian gardens in this wonderful guide harness the high, wild countryside around them. They create a counterpoint of meticulous planting against a background of grandeur. The scale of the individual bloom set against one of the great European landscapes.

The Lake District is not wilderness. It's a landscape with the stamp of man and has been since the first stone axe maker set up in business on the Langdale Pikes five and a half thousand years ago. The great gardens introduced here are another creative chapter in that continuing story.

Eric Robson

Blackwell, The Arts & Crafts House Cumbria

An architectural gem set amidst stunning views of the lake and mountains, Blackwell is one of the most important and rare surviving Arts and Crafts Movement houses in England. Originally built in 1900 as a holiday home, today Blackwell is the only example of the architect M H Baillie Scott's work open to the public. Amazingly, the carved oak panelling, wrought ironwork, Art Nouveau stained glass, intricate plasterwork, stone carving and original fireplaces with William De Morgan tiling have all survived intact.

The gardens were cleverly designed by Thomas Mawson in a series of terraces, bordered by beautiful flower beds with climbing plants and exotic herbs, to make the most of the breathtaking views. This is one of the loveliest places anywhere in England to sit outside and enjoy morning coffee, lunch or afternoon tea overlooking Windermere Lake and Coniston Fells.

Fact File

Opening Times:	7th February - 23rd December 2005
Admission Rates:	Adults £5.00 (2005), Discounts for children and families.
Groups Rates:	Minimum group size 10
	Special rates for pre-booked groups and school groups.
Facilities:	Craft and Book Shop, Tearoom, Changing Exhibitions.
Disabled Access:	Partial. Toilets and parking for disabled on site. Wheelchair available for loan. Booking advisable.
Tours/Events:	Please telephone for details.
Coach Parking:	Free coach parking available for pre-booked groups, close to the site.
Length of Visit:	2 hours
Booking Contact:	Catriona Sale
	Blackwell, the Arts & Crafts House, Bowness-On-Windermere, Cumbria LA23 3JR
	Telephone: 015394 46139 Fax: 015394 88486
Email:	info@blackwell.org.uk
Website:	www.blackwell.org.uk
Location:	M6 J36, Blackwell is situated 1 1/2 miles south of Bowness-on-Windermere just off the A5074 on the B5360.

Please quote this guide when booking

Brantwood's gardens and estate are like no other. Mature Victorian landscape gardens lead to Ruskin's own experimental landscapes, to ancient woodlands, high Moorland and spectacular views. Completion of the Zig-Zaggy, a garden begun by John Ruskin 130 years ago, and the High Walk, a spectacular Victorian viewing platform, brings a total of eight gardens restored at Brantwood. Expect the unexpected and explore 250 acres of fascinating landscape.

Whichever season you choose to visit you are assured year round interest. Spectacular azaleas in springtime; a collection of ferns, herbs and colourful herbaceous borders in summer; the vibrant colours of autumn; or a winter snowfall can transform the gardens into a winter wonderland.

Stroll the paths, sit and marvel at the magnificent views. Whatever you choose to do, you will take home with you the discovery of John Ruskin's legacy and inspiration.

Fact File

Opening Times:	Mid - March to mid - November daily 11am - 5.30pm.
	Mid - November to mid - March Wednesday - Sunday 11am - 4.30pm.
Admission Rates:	Adults £5.50 / £3.75 garden only, Child £1.00
Groups Rates:	Minimum group size: 10
	Adults £4.50 / £3.00 garden only, Child £1.00
Facilities:	Shop, Plant Sales, Restaurant, Craft Gallery.
Disabled Access:	Partial. Toilet and parking for disabled on site. Wheelchairs on loan, booking necessary.
Tours/Events:	A wide variety of events await, please check website for details.
Coach Parking:	Yes but limited.
Length of Visit:	4 - 6 hours
Booking Contact:	Josie Coombe
	Brantwood, Coniston, Cumbria, LA21 8AD
	Telephone: 01539 441396 Fax: 01539 441263
Email:	josie@brantwood.org.uk
Website:	www.brantwood.org.uk
Location:	2 1/4 miles east of Coniston. Signposted from Coniston.

Please quote this guide when booking

Dalemain Historic House & Gardens   Cumbria

Come to Dalemain to enjoy the delightful and fascinating 5-acre plantsman's garden set against the picturesque splendour of the Lakeland Fells and parkland. Walk around the richly planted herbaceous borders, the rose walk with nearly 200 old fashioned roses. The garden also features a magnificent *Abies Cephalonica*, a Tudor Knot Garden and a wild Garden with a profusion of flowering shrubs and wild flowers. In early summer, enjoy the breathtaking display of blue Himalayan Poppies. Take in the views on the glorious woodland walk high above the Dacre Beck. The gardens have been featured on *BBC TV Gardener's World* and in *Country Life* and *English Garden*.

Dalemain is a much-loved family home with history stretching from Saxon times to early Georgian. You can also enjoy visiting the House, Museums, Shop and Tearoom.

Fact File

Opening Times:	20th March - 30th October 2005
Admission Rates:	House & Garden - Adults £6.00, Senior Citizens £6.00, Accompanied Child Free
	Garden only - Adults £4.00, Senior Citizen £4.00, Accompanied Child Free
Groups Rates:	Minimum group size 10
	House & Garden - Adults £4.50, Senior Citizen £4.50, Accompanied Child Free
	Garden only - Adults £3.50, Senior Citizen £3.50, Accompanied Child Free
Facilities:	Gift Shop, Plant Sales, Tearoom & Licensed Restaurant, Museums.
Disabled Access:	Partial. Toilets and parking for disabled on site. Wheelchairs on loan. Booking Advisable.
Tours/Events:	Please call for details
Coach Parking:	Yes
Length of Visit:	1 - 4 Hours
Booking Contact:	Jennifer Little
	Dalemain Historic House & Gardens, Dalemain, Penrith, Cumbria. CA11 0HB
	Telephone: 017684 86450 Fax: 017684 86223
Email:	admin@dalemain.com
Website:	www@dalemain.com
Location:	On the A592 Penrith to Ullswater, 3 miles from M6 - J40

Please quote this guide when booking

Holker Hall is a superb Victorian house built on a grand scale in a style best described as neo-Elizabethan. It is the home of Lord and Lady Cavendish, and despite the richness of the interior this is very much a family home. Visitors are made to feel like welcome guests rather than tourists.

The Gardens surrounding Holker Hall cover 25 acres of woodland and formal garden areas. Winner of the 2004 "Cumbria in Bloom" Award for Horticultural Excellence, they are highly acclaimed and offer a richness and variety particular to this special micro-climate of the South Lakes. Throughout the year the Gardens are a riot of colour and texture. Special Garden Tours are conducted every Thursday at 2:00pm. Bespoke Garden tours can be arranged upon request and can be tailored to suit the varied interests of the visitor. The 17th century Holker Lime measuring 7'6" at its widest, was awarded the honour of being one of Britain's 50 greatest trees. Another rare treat during the summer, around the time of the Garden Festival is the blooming of the National collection of styracaeae. Not forgetting the Rhododendrons in the months of April and May and the colours of the Autumn Gardens will thrill and excite even the most discerning.

Fact File

Opening Times: Hall & Gardens - 20th March - 30th October (Closed Saturdays) Gates open at 10.30am - 4.45pm (Hall Closes) 5.30pm (Garden Closes).
All other facilities open daily from 1st March.

Admission Rates: Hall, Gardens & Motor Museum, Adults £9.25, Child £5.50.

Group Rates: Minimum group size: 20, please call for details.

Facilities: The Holker Food Hall, Courtyard Cafe, Gift Shop.

Disabled Access: Yes. Toilet and parking for disabled on site. Wheelchairs on loan. booking necessary.

Tours/Events: The Garden Festival at Holker Hall June 3rd, 4th & 5th, Bespoke garden tours available.

Coach Parking: Yes

Length of Visit: 2 - 4 hours

Booking Contact: Elizabeth M Ward
Holker Hall, Cark-in-Cartmel, Nr Grange-over-Sands, Cumbria, LA11 7PR
Telephone: 015395 58328 Fax: 015395 58378

Email: publicopening@holker.co.uk

Website: www.holker-hall.co.uk

Location: New M6 junction 36, follow Brown & White Tourist signs through Grange-over-Sands.

Please quote this guide when booking

The Terraces which run down from the southern and western sides of the house are 17th century, though the steps and walls were designed by William Sawrey Gilpin and Anthony Salvin in the 1820s. The clipped yews are late 19th century, reflecting the Arts and Crafts revival of interest in topiary.

The Low Garden was a formal rhododendron garden laid out in 1870. The design of the paths is based on the form of two interlocking stars.

In the 17th century the Walled Garden on the north side of the house was an ornamental Dutch Garden. The walls were built by Henry Fletcher in 1736 and there are records of a large number of fruit trees which were planted then. In the last few years an increasing collection of herbaceous plants has transformed the Walled Garden into a beautiful summer garden.

The Woodland Walk surrounding the gardens includes 65 types of tree and a 17th century dovecote.

Fact File

Opening Times:	Gardens daily (except Saturdays) - 25th March - 31st October 2005.
Admission Rates:	Gardens only, Adults £3.00, Senior Citizen £3.00, Child Free.
Groups Rates:	Minimum group size: 20
	Gardens only. Adults £2.50, Senior Citizen £2.50, Child Free.
Facilities:	Gift Shop, Teas, When House is open (Thu, Fri, Sun & B H Mon).
Disabled Access:	Partial. Parking for disabled on site. Electric Wheelchair on loan.
Tours/Events:	Please call for details.
Coach Parking:	Yes
Length of Visit:	1 1/2 Hours (with House 3 hours)
Booking Contact:	Edward Thompson
	Hutton-in-the-Forest, Penrith, Cumbria, CA11 9TH
	Telephone: 017684 84449 Fax: 017684 84571
Email:	info@hutton-in-the-forest.co.uk
Website:	www.hutton-in-the-forest.co.uk
Location:	2 1/2 miles North West of M6 Junction 41 on B5305 towards Wigton;
	6 miles from Penrith.

Please quote this guide when booking

Original garden laid out C.1694 by Monsieur Guillame Beaumont. Yew trees sculptured into cones, corkscrews, circles and other curious shapes, interspersed with impeccably-clipped box and colourful herbaceous borders make Levens Hall's topiary garden unique in Britain. Fountain Garden, Potager and Herb Garden, Rose Garden, wall borders, orchards, trees, shrubs and lawns. The earliest ha-ha. Overlooking the gardens is the Elizabethan House which contains a fine collection of jacobean furniture, plasterwork and panelling.

"Not even David Beckham's barnet gets that much attention." Sunday Times.
"I didn't think I liked topiary untill I went to Levens." Rosie Atkins, Curator Chelsea Physic Garden.
"Totally eccentric and truly memorable." Dan Pearson, Gardening correspondent, Sunday Times.
"The most amazing topiary, one of the World's best". Sunday Times.
"Yew and box hedges which wouldn't be out of place on the set of an Alice in Wonderland movie". Sunday Times.
"One of the world's Great Gardens". Sunday Times.
"Considered to be in the top ten U.K. Gardens." Monty Don.

Fact File

Opening Times:	Tuesday 12th April - Thursday 13th October.
Admission Rates:	House & Gardens (Gardens Only) Adults £8.00(£5.90),Child £3.80 (£2.70).
Groups Rates:	Minimum group size: 20
	Adults £5.00, Child £2.50.
Facilities:	Gift Shop, Plant Sales, Tearoom, Levens Hall.
Disabled Access:	Yes (Not House). Parking for disabled on site. Wheelchairs on loan, booking necessary.
Tours/Events:	None
Coach Parking:	Yes
Length of Visit:	2 Hours
Booking Contact:	Levens Hall, Kendal, Cumbria LA8 0PD
	Telephone: 015395 60321 Fax: 015395 60669
Email:	email@levenshall.fsnet.co.uk
Website:	www.levenshall.co.uk
Location:	Junction 36 of M6, Oxenholme railway station.

Please quote this guide when booking

Muncaster

Set in the dramatic grandeur of the Lakeland Fells, the wild, woodland gardens are home to an incredible collection of rare and beautiful plants. Miles of paths wind through this extra-ordinary scenery, which also provides cover for a varied wildlife population. A great plant-hunting tradition flourishes at Muncaster and many of the plants in the gardens are now highly endangered in their native habitats due to population pressures and deforestation. Thousands of specimens, particularly from China and the Far East, have been grown from seed collected on recent expeditions around the turn of the Third Millennium. British plants too flourish in abundance, and the bluebells in the high woods should not be missed in late April and early May. Gardens evolve and change, and no matter what time of year you visit, there is always something in flower and new discoveries to be made, and the highlight: the view from the Castle and Terrace is truly "Heaven's Gate" as described by John Ruskin, the 19th Century father of the conservation movement.

Fact File

Opening Times:	14th February - 6th November open daily 10.30am.
Admission Rates:	Adults £6.00, Child £4.00, Family £18.00.
Group Rates:	Minimum group size: 12
	Adults £5.50, Child £3.00.
Facilities:	3 Shops, Cafe, Play Area for children.
Disabled Access:	Partial. Toilet and parking for disabled on site. Electric Wheelchair on loan, booking necessary
Tours/Events:	Festival of Rhododendrons, Camellias & Azaleas (April - May),
	Bluebell Heaven - (April - May), R H S Lecture Sat 7th May 2005.
Coach Parking:	Yes
Length of Visit:	3 1/2 hours
Booking Contact:	Joanne Hall
	Muncaster Castle, Ravenglass, Cumbria, CA18 1RQ
	Telephone: 01229 717614 Fax: 01229 717010
Email:	info@muncaster.co.uk
Website:	www.muncaster.co.uk
Location:	1 mile south of Ravenglass.

Please quote this guide when booking

37

Nestling between the beautiful fells, Lake Windermere and Rydal Water are the famous 'romantic' gardens of Rydal Mount, home of William Wordsworth from 1813 - 1850. The gardens landscaped by the poet have changed little since his day. He believed that a garden should be informal and at one with nature and the surrounding countryside. They consist of fell-sided terraces, herbaceous borders, rock pools and an ancient Norse mound. There are rare shrubs and in season, the daffodils, blue bells and rhododendrons produce a spectacular display of colour.

Experience this delightful garden and enjoy the peaceful and relaxed atmosphere of the lived in family home. Here the poet wrote and revised many of his famous poems including the world renowned **Daffodils** and became poet laureate to Queen Victoria.

'O happy gardens! Whose seclusion deep, so friendly to industrious hours;........ *William Wordsworth.*

Fact File

Opening Times:	Summer: March to October 9.30am - 5pm, Winter: November to February 10am - 4pm (Closed - Tues in Winter, 8th Jan - 1st Feb and Christmas Day).
Admission Rates:	House & Garden (Garden only) - Adults £4.50 (£2.00), Senior Citizen £3.75 (£2.00) Child £1.50 (5-15yrs).
Groups Rates:	Minimum group size 10 House & Garden (Garden only) - Adults £3.50 (£2.00) Child £1.50 (5-15yrs).
Facilities:	Gift Shop.
Disabled Access:	Partial, parking for disabled on site.
Tours/Events:	None
Coach Parking:	Yes
Length of Visit:	1 - 1 1/2 hours.
Booking Contact:	Marian Elkington Rydal Mount & Gardens, Rydal Nr Ambleside, Cumbria, LA22 9LU. Tel: 015394 33002 Fax: 015394 31738
Email:	rydalmount@aol.com
Website:	www.rydalmount.co.uk
Location:	1 1/2 miles from Ambleside on the A591 Windermere to Keswick Road. Free Parking.

Please quote this guide when booking

Sizergh Castle

Cumbria

Sizergh Castle, originally built in the Middle Ages by the Strickland family, who still live there today, has magnificent furniture and treasures and is surrounded by a wonderful garden with a lake and superb rock garden. There is also a kitchen garden with vegetables, herbs, cut flowers and soft fruits. All this is set in a 1600 acre, estate crossed by public footpaths, providing short walks from the castle to dramatic viewpoints over Morecambe Bay and the Lake District fells.

The imposing Castle has an exceptional series of oak-panelled rooms. One of the best rooms is the Inlaid Chamber. Portraits, fine furniture and ceramics collected over the centuries by the family are shown alongside their recent photographs.

Fact File

Opening Times: 23rd March - 30th October 2005
Admission Rates: House & Garden (Garden only) Adults £5.80 (£3.00), Child £2.90. (£1.70).
Group Rates: Minimum group size: 15 - Adults £4.80.
Facilities: Gift Shop, Tea Room, Plant Sales.
Disabled Access: Partial. Toilet and parking for disabled on site, Wheelchairs on loan Booking Advisable
Tours/Events: None.
Coach Parking: Yes.
Length of Visit: 2 1/2 hours.
Booking Contact: Administrator
The National Trust, Sizergh Castle and Garden, Sizergh, Nr Kendal. Cumbria, LA8 8AE
Tel: 015395 60951 Fax: 015395 60951
Email: sizergh@nationaltrust.org.uk
Website: www.nationaltrust .org.uk
Location: J 36 of the M6, then A590 Kendal direction. Take Barrow-in-Furness turning off and follow brown signs.
From Lake District, follow A591 South M6 direction. Turn off towards Barrow-in-Furness (A590) and follow brown signs.

Please quote this guide when booking

Spanning nearly 300 years of horticultural history, Bicton Park Botanical Gardens are set in the picturesque Otter Valley, Where the gentle climate ensures a magnificent display of exotic plants throughout the year. From the classical grandeur of the 18th century Italian Garden, Bicton's 63 acres (25.5 ha) extend through less formal gardens to a superbly landscaped parkland with lakes, streams, a nature trail and Devon's largest collection of record-holding trees. Twenty five conifers and broadleaf specimens have been officially recognised as the tallest or the largest of their kind in the British Isles. Bicton's 19th Century Palm House is one of the world's most beautiful garden buildings. Many other tropical plants and cacti are also displayed under cover, as are the fascinating exhibits in the Countryside Museum and Shell House. For a small extra charge, visitors may tour Bicton Park on Britain's only 18-inch gauge passenger-carrying railway.

Fact File

Opening Times: Daily all year (except Christmas Day & Boxing Day) from 10am - 6pm in spring/summer and 10am - 5pm in autumn/winter.

Admission Rates: Adults £5.95 Senior Citizen £4.95, Child £4.95, Family (2 Adults+2 Children) £19.95, Dogs £1.00.

Groups Rate: Minimum group size: 16
Adults £3.95, Senior Citizen £3.95, Child £2.95

Facilities: Restaurant, Gift Shop, Garden Centre, Kiosk's, picnic area, children's indoor and outdoor play areas, mini-golf course.

Disabled Access: Yes. Toilet and parking for disabled on site. Wheelchairs on loan by prior arrangement.

Tours/Events: Walks for groups by prior arrangement. Tours may be tailored to your special interests, including history, trees, wildlife.

Coach Parking: Yes   **Length of Visit:** 3 hours minimum all day max

Booking Contact: Heather / Valerie / Simon. Bicton Park Botanical Gardens, East Budleigh, Budleigh Salterton, Devon, EX9 7BJ Telephone: 01395 568465 Fax: 01395 568374

Email: simon@bictongardens.co.uk **Website:** www.bictongardens.co.uk

Location: Bicton is 10 miles SE of Exeter. From M5 leave at junction 30 and follow the brown 'Bicton Park' signs. The gardens are midway between Budleigh Salterton and Newton Poppleford on the B3178.

Please quote this guide when booking

The eighteenth-century landscape garden and park, leading away from the magnificent Palladian House, was created by the 1st Lord Fortescue in 1730 with temples, follies, ponds and across the valley a Triumphal Arch. At the top of the hill above the house is a Castle (complete with cannons) from which Dartmoor, Exmoor and Lundy Island are visible on a clear day. The spring woodland garden shelters magnolias, camellias, rhododendrons, azaleas, a 2 acre daffodil wood, and thousands of bulbs, with some rare and renowned trees in the Easter Close. The summer Millennium garden designed by Xa Tollemache has herbaceous borders planted with lillies, agapanthus, phlox and penstemon edged with box and lavender in gentle curves lining gravel paths plus a spectacular water sculpture by Giles Rayner.

Fact File

Opening Times: 25th March - 29th August Inc. (Sun, Mon, Wed and Fri)
Admission Rates: Adults £4.00, Senior Citizens £4.00, Child & Disabled Free.
Group Rates: None.
Facilities: Occasional Plant Sales.
Disabled Access: Partial, Toilet and parking for disabled on site.
Tours/Events: Guided tours 20 people minimum £25.00 per guide. Filleigh fete 20 August 2005.
Coach Parking: Yes.
Length of Visit: 1 - 2 hours
Booking Contact: Margaret Pine
Castle Hill, Filleigh, Barnstaple, Devon, EX32 ORQ
Telephone: 01598 760336 (Ext 4) Fax: 01598 760457
Email: ladyarran@castlehill-devon.com
Website: None
Location: Leave A361 at roundabout west of South Molton, follow signs to Filleigh. Shortly after passing through Stagshead, yellow lodge on the right. Go through drive gates following signs to car park.

Please quote this guide when booking

Escot Fantasy Gardens, Maze & Woodland — Devon

Escot is unique. Originally laid out in the 18th century as 220 acres of 'Capability Brown' parkland and gardens, contemporary design elements have been added by Ivan Hicks, the well-known TV Gardener-artist. In between, generations of the Kennaway family have travelled the world bringing a wide range of shrubs and magnificent champion trees. Woodland paths and trails now lead visitors to the remarkable new Beech Hedge Maze with its five hedge-leaping bridges and stunning central look-out tower; to the birds of prey with their summertime displays; through the beginnings of an International Tree Foundation wood, carpeted with beautiful flowers in Spring; through the wild boar and otter enclosures; to an award-winning aquatic centre and a dedicated wetlands conservation area.

As a final stop, the Coach House Restaurant serves delicious home-cooked food using the very best local produce.

Escot is refreshingly uncommercial and, indeed, unique.

Fact File

Opening Times: All year except 25th & 26th December

Admission Rates: Adults £5.50, Senior Citizen £4.00, Child £4.00 (3-15yrs) under 3yrs Free.

Groups Rates: Minimum group size: 10
Adults £5.00, Senior Citizen £3.50, Child £3.50 (3-15yrs) under 3yrs Free.

Facilities: Gift Shop, Plant Sales, Teas, Restaurant, Aquatic & Pet Centre, Maze, Birds of Prey displays, International Tree Foundation Wood, West Country Rivers Trust Demonstration Site, Dedicated Wetlands Conservation Area.

Disabled Access: Partial. Toilet and parking for disabled on site.

Tours/Events: Please call for details.

Coach Parking: Yes

Length of Visit: 3 - 4 Hours + meals

Booking Contact: Mr & Mrs J M Kennaway (Owners)
Escot, Ottery St Mary, Devon, EX11 1LU.
Telephone: 01404 822188 Fax: 01404 822903

Email: escot@eclipse.co.uk

Website: www.escot-devon.co.uk

Location: See Website for Map - Escot is just off the A30 Exeter to Honiton road at Fairmile. (Follow brown signs).

Please quote this guide when booking

Heddon Hall Gardens North Devon

Gardening is on a grand scale at Heddon Hall.

Since 1990, a knowledgeable and experienced gardener has created 5 acres of horticultural delights. Set in an intimate valley the Georgian house is surrounded by a formal terrace with climbers and generously planted borders. Through a quiet courtyard is an explosion of colour from a hot bed, and beyond is a beautiful walled garden, the layout by Penelope Hobhouse, with clipped box hedges, old English roses, cordoned apple trees, flowers, herbs and vegetables.

Many rare plants and trees flourish here, having been bought back from Jane Keatley's plant hunting trips abroad. A secret garden abundant with themed beds of herbaceous plants leads to a steep less formal natural rockery, where the River Heddon tumbles down to the sea via 3 stew ponds, recently renovated.

Many well known gardeners have contributed to the garden, including Carol Klein.

Fact File

Opening Times:	May 1st - July 31st, Afternoons only 2pm - 5.30pm Sunday, Wednesday, Friday and Bank Holidays.
Admission Rates:	Adults £3.50, Senior Citizens £3.50, Child free under 14s
Group Rates:	Minimum group size: 10
	Adults £2.50, Senior Citizens £2.50. Child free under 14s
Facilities:	Homemade Teas, Plant Sales
Disabled Access:	Yes (garden gravel), parking for disabled on site (limited).
Tours/Events:	None
Coach Parking:	Yes (larger coaches by arrangement).
Length of Visit:	2 - 3 1/2 hours
Booking Contact:	Mr & Mrs F De Falbe
	Heddon Hall, Parracombe, Barnstaple, North Devon EX31 4QL
	Telephone: 01598 763541 Fax: 01598 763541
Email:	Juliet@camwest.co.uk
Website:	None.
Location:	SS67 45 Barnstaple Lynton Road A39, 400 yds up the hill from village centre, drive is situated on the right hand side.

Please quote this guide when booking

Set deep in the lovely North Devon countryside, RHS Garden Rosemoor has now come of age as a garden of national importance. Lady Anne Berry gifted Rosemoor to the RHS 16 years ago, since then the original eight acres have been greatly developed.

To the huge range of plants collected by Lady Anne, the RHS has added features such as the Formal Garden, extensive herbaceous borders, herb and cottage gardens, a potager, the Foliage and Plantsman's Garden and extensive stream and lakeside plantings. Recent additions include the Mediterranean and semi-tropical plantings which have been thriving during the recent long hot summers and the newly planted Winter Garden. But what is perhaps the most popular feature of this delightful garden is the extensive rose garden, proving beyond doubt the lie that the West Country cannot produce beautiful roses.

"Voted South West Visitor Attraction of the Year 2003".

Fact File

Opening Times: April - September 10am-6pm, October - March 10am - 5pm, open every day except Christmas Day. Visitor Centre Closed noon Christmas eve and re-opens 10am 27th Dec.

Admission Rates: Adults £5.50, Senior Citizen £5.50, Child £1.50, RHS Members Free

Group Rates: Minimum group size: 10
Adults £4.50, Senior Citizen £4.50, Child £1.50.

Facilities: Visitor Centre, Shop, Restaurant, Wisteria Tea Room, Plant Sales.

Disabled Access: Yes. Toilet and Parking for disabled on site. Wheelchairs on loan, booking necessary.

Tours/Events: Full programme of events throughout the year.

Coach Parking: Yes

Length of Visit: 2 hours

Booking Contact: Helen Foster-Collins
RHS Garden Rosemoor, Great Torrington, North Devon, EX38 8PH
Telephone 01805 624067 Fax: 01805 624717

Email: helenfostercollins@rhs.org.uk

Website: www.rhs.org.uk

Location: 1 mile south of Torrington on the A3124 (formerly B3220)

Please quote this guide when booking

Abbotsbury Sub Tropical Gardens   Dorset

Established in 1765 by the first Countess of Ilchester. Developed since then into a 20-acre grade 1 listed magnificent woodland valley garden. World famous for it's Camellia Groves, Magnolias, Rhododendron and Hydrangea collections. In summer it is awash with colour.

Since the restoration after the great storm of 1990 many new and exotic plants have been introduced. The garden is now a mixture of formal and informal, with a charming walled garden and spectacular woodland valley views.

Facilities include a Colonial Tea House for lunches, snacks and drinks, a Plant Centre and quality Gift Shop. Events such as Shakespeare and concerts are presented during the year. The Floodlighting of the Garden at the end of October should not be missed.

Fact File

Opening Times:	Summer: 10am - 6pm last entry at 5pm.
	Winter (November - February) - 10.00am - 4pm or dusk, last entry 1 hour before.
Admission Rates:	Adults £6.80, Senior Citizen £6.00, Child £4.00
Groups Rates:	Minimum group size 10
	Adults £5.80, Senior Citizen £5.00, Child £3.00
Facilities:	Colonial Tea House, Gift Shop, Plant Centre.
Disabled Access:	Yes. 50% of garden accessible. Toilet and parking for disabled on site. Wheelchairs F.O.C.
Tours/Events:	£1 per person (minimum charge £20) on top of the group rate (minimum 10 people).
	Special events see web site.
Coach Parking:	Yes
Length of Visit:	2 hours
Booking Contact:	Jess Owen. Abbotsbury Sub Tropical Garden, Bullers Way, Abbotsbury, (Nr Weymouth), Dorset, DT3 4LA. Telephone: 01305 871130 Fax: 01305 871092
Email:	info@abbotsbury-tourism.co.uk
Website:	www.abbotsbury-tourism.co.uk
Location:	On the B3157 between Weymouth and Bridport in Dorset. come off the A35 near Dorchester at Wintervorne Abbas.

Please quote this guide when booking

The contemporary parkland and pleasure gardens were laid out in the "Jardin Anglais" style popularised by Capability Brown, which consisted of rolling turf, carefully placed groups of trees and a lake. The lovely 35 acre formal gardens were created between 1915 and 1922 within the existing framework of the 18th Century Parkland setting. The gardens have undergone an extensive programme of restoration with new plantings rich in variety and interest. Gardens are not static and Kingston Maurward, like all good gardens, is constantly evolving.

The Animal Park is a firm favourite with children and home to an interesting collection of animals. There is a large play area and plenty of space for picnics. The Visitor Centre provides information on the Animal Park and Gardens and has a wide variety of plants and gifts for sale.

Fact File

Opening Times: 5th January to 21st December 10am - 5.30pm.
Admission Rates: Adults £4.00, Senior Citizen £4.00, Child £2.50.
Group Rates: Minimum group size: 10
Adults £3.50, Senior Citizen £3.50, Child £2.50.
Facilities: Visitor Centre, Shop, Tea Room, Plant Sales, Picnic Area
Children's Play Area, Animal Park.
Disabled Access: Yes. Toilet & parking for disabled on site. Wheelchairs on loan, booking necessary.
Tours/Events: Guided walks are available if booked in advance.
Special events take place throughout the year, telephone for details.
Coach Parking: Yes
Length of Visit: Minimum 2 hours
Booking Contact: Ginny Rolls
Kingston Maurward, Dorchester, Dorset, DT2 8PY
Telephone 01305 215003 Fax: 01305 215001
Email: events@kmc.ac.uk
Website: www.kmc.ac.uk/gardens
Location: Signposted from the roundabout at the eastern end of the Dorchester by-pass A35.

Please quote this guide when booking

Stapehill is a superb venue for group visits, offering a wide range of attractions to suit people of all tastes and ages for one admission price. The glorious award winning gardens, including the stunning Japanese Garden stocked with beautiful koi carp are a joy to behold. The 12,000 sq.ft museum with it's artisan workshops tells the history of farming through Victorian England. The 19th Century Cistercian Abbey houses the crafts people and has the Nuns Chapel, Cloisters and Cloister Garden plus the history of the Abbey, all this creates a truly unique experience, and with all but the gardens under cover, even the weather cannot spoil a memorable day at Stapehill.

The lovely licensed coffee shop provides morning coffee, light lunches, afternoon, and cream teas. Special events are held throughout the year including craft fairs, flower and garden festival and our magical Christmas weekends.

Fact File

Opening Times:	Daily 10am - 5pm Easter - September. Wednesday - Sunday 10am - 4pm October - Easter. Closed Christmas Holiday and all of January.
Admission Rates:	Adults £7.50, Senior Citizen £7.00, Child £4.50
Groups Rate:	Minimum group size: 15 Adults £6.00, Senior Citizen £5.50, Child £4.00
Facilities:	Visitor Centre, Shop, Plant Sales, Teas, Licensed Coffee Shop with home-made quiches and other light lunches.
Disabled Access:	Yes. Toilet and Parking for disabled on site.
Tours/Events:	All year - please call for details
Coach Parking:	Yes
Length of Visit:	2 1/2 plus hours (all weather attraction)
Booking Contact:	Mrs Sheena Tinsdale. Stapehill Abbey, 276 Wimborne Road West, Stapehill, Wimborne, Dorset, BH21 2EB. Telephone: 01202 861686 Fax: 01202 894589
Email:	None
Website:	None
Location:	2 1/2 miles east of the Historic town of Wimborne Minster. Just off A31 at Canford Bottom roundabout.

Please quote this guide when booking

Cressing Temple Barns   Essex

Enter the Tudor Walled Garden at Cressing Temple and you step back in time. The plants that grow here are those that would have been available in the Tudor period; the design, a result of painstaking research and archeological excavation.

Within the Tudor walls of the Garden are themed areas, with borders devoted to medicinal, culinary and dyers' plants, a potager and nuttery. The nosegay garden is a fragrant delight with its wealth of sweetly scented plants, grown in the period for their perfume. The arbour is planted to recall Shakespeare's Midsummer Night's Dream with a profusion of roses, woodbine and oxlips.

The Walled Garden nestles to the side of one of the two magnificent medieval Barns for which Cressing Temple is renowned. These date to the early 13th century, a time when the site was owned by the mysterious Knights Templar.

Fact File

Opening Times: 6th March - 30th October - Sundays 10.30am - 5pm, 4th May - 30th September - Wed/Thurs/Fri 10.30am - 4.30pm. Please note opening times are being reviewed and will be extended. Closed - Good Friday, Easter Saturday, Open Easter Sunday and Monday 10.30 - 4.30pm.

Admission Rates: Adults £3.50, Senior Citizen £2.50, Child £2.50 (under 3yrs free). Family (2+3) £8.50.

Group Rates: 10% discount on groups over 15

Facilities: Gift shop, Plant Sales, Tea Room, Medieval Barns & Exhibition. Audio Tours (from April) Tour guides Sundays or on request.

Disabled Access: Yes. Toilet and parking for disabled on site. Wheelchairs on loan.

Tours/Events: Various events through the year, for details call or see our website.

Coach Parking: Yes

Length of Visit: 1 1/2 - 2 hours

Booking Contact: Colleen Coles, Witham Road, Braintree, Essex, CM77 8PD
Telephone: 01376 584903 Fax: 01376 584864

Email: cressing.temple.org.uk

Website: www.cressingtemple.org.uk

Location: From A12 take Witham turn off, then follow signs to Braintree, Cressing Temple is on the B1018. From A120 follow brown signs towards Freeport, Cressing Temple is sign posted.

Please quote this guide when booking

The Gibberd Garden　　　　　　　　　　　　Essex

The garden is a highly individual creation of Sir Frederick Gibberd, Master planner for Harlow new town. It is sited on the side of a small valley which slopes down to a brook. Occupying some seven acres, the garden was planned as a series of 'rooms', each with its own character. The glades, pools and alleys provide settings for some fifty sculptures, large ceramic pots, architectural salvage, a gazebo and even a children's moated castle with a drawbridge! Jane Brown, the garden and landscape design writer, has described it as "one of the few outstanding examples of 20th Century garden design".

The Gibberd Garden Trust aims to realise Sir Frederick's wish that the garden sould be open to the public for study and relaxation. It has been acquired with the generous help of the Heritage Lottery Fund and is currently undergoing an imaginative and extensive restoration programme.

Fact File

Opening Times:	2pm to 6pm Wednesdays, Saturdays, Sundays & Bank Holidays. Beginning April to end September.
Admission Rates:	Adults £4.00, Concessions £2.50, Child Free if accompanied
Group Rates:	Minimum group size: 10 (As above during open times) One free entry in 10. Please telephone for details at other times.
Facilities:	Visitor Centre, Shop, Teas.
Disabled Access:	Restricted. Toilet and parking for disabled on site.
Tours/Events:	None.
Coach Parking:	Please telephone to make arrangements (restricted access, 33 seater only).
Length of Visit:	2 hours
Booking Contact:	Mrs Jane Quinton The Gibberd Garden, Marsh Lane, Gilden Way, Harlow, Essex, CM17 0NA Telephone: 01279 442112
Email:	None
Website:	www.thegibberdgarden.co.uk
Location:	Off B183 Harlow to Hatfield Heath Road. Brown Signs.

Please quote this guide when booking

RHS Garden Hyde Hall

Essex

Situated in the heart of Essex farmland in Rettendon to the south of Chelmsford, RHS Garden Hyde Hall is the perfect place to discover the real Essex. With countryside views so rarely associated with this part of England, Hyde Hall is a palate of sumptuous rich and varied colours providing inspiration for the novice and keen gardener alike. Just 40 miles from London, this haven of peace and tranquillity provides the perfect day out. Now open all year round, recent work in the garden has focused on introducing planting and design that will captivate and inspire visitors throughout the seasons.

Throughout the year an extensive range of courses, workshops and special events are organised, with the aim of both enriching a visit to the garden, but also to encourage adults and children to try their hand at something new. The thriving schools programme provides education for any age group, the onsite Education Officer working with teachers to cover a range of subjects linked to the National Curriculum.

Fact File

Opening Times:	**Now open all year** (except for Christmas Day) 10am to 6pm (5pm or dusk Oct - Mar) Last entry one hour before closing.
Admission Rates:	Adults £4.50, Child £1.00.
Groups Rates:	Minimum group size 10 + pre-booked Adults £3.50 - RHS member + one guest free. (Free meal voucher for coach driver)
Facilities:	Plant Centre & Gift Shop, Licensed Barn Restaurant, Visitor Centre, Garden Library.
Disabled Access:	Most areas. Parking, toilet facilities and ramped access to Barn Restaurant.
Tours/Events:	On-going programme of events throughout the year, including Summer Festival Fortnight, Apple Festival and new for 2005, a Lavender Weekend. Contact garden direct for a copy of the Events Programme.
Coach Parking:	Yes
Length of Visit:	3 - 4 hours
Booking Contact:	Jane Kernan, Group Bookings Administrator, RHS Garden Hyde Hall, Buckhatch Lane, Rettendon, Chelmsford, Essex CM3 8ET. Telephone : 01245 400256 Fax; 01245 402100
Email:	hydehall@rhs.org.uk **Website:** www.rhs.org.uk
Location:	South-east of Chelmsford, Brown tourism signed from A130.

Please quote this guide when booking

The newly redesigned Walled Garden at Marks Hall was greeted with great enthusiasm when it opened in 2003.

The five individual gardens and the double long border are a unique blend of traditional and contemporary, combining unusual landscaping and creative and colourful planting. This garden is at its best from early summer through to autumn but on the opposite lake bank there is the Millennium Walk designed to be at its best in the shortest days of the year. Here the stems of dogwood, rubus and birch reflect in the lake and the scent of Hamamelis lingers.

There is much more to see in this Arboretum and Garden of over 100 acres and new plantings mature and surprise each year.

Fact File

Opening Times:	Tuesday - Sunday 10.30am - 5pm, Bank Holdiays and winter weekends.
Admission Rates:	£4.00 per car.
Groups Rates:	Minimum group size 12 £2.00 per person
Facilities:	Visitor Centre, Shop, Plant Sales, Teas, Restaurant.
Disabled Access:	Yes. Toilet and parking for disabled on site. Wheelchairs and buggy on loan.
Tours/Events:	Please telephone for details.
Coach Parking:	Yes
Length of Visit:	2 1/2 hours
Booking Contact:	Marian Ripper Marks Hall, Coggeshall, Essex, CO6 1TG Tel: 01376 563796 Fax: 01376 563132
Email:	marian@markshall.org.uk
Website:	www.markshall.org.uk
Location:	Signed from A120 Coggeshall by-pass.

Please quote this guide when booking

Barton House   Gloucestershire

The six acres of garden surrounding this Cotswolds manor house which was remodelled by Inigo Jones in 1636 offer many varied features and surprises. Huge Rhododendron borders (the only ones in the Cotswolds) greet the visitor. Rhododendrons are in flower from Christmas to the late autumn. The trees are either mature, dating from 1850 - Scots Pines, Wellingtonias, Douglas Firs, Copper Beeches etc - or Cedars, Paulownias, over 30 Magnolias, collections of Stuartias, Nothofagus and Eucryphias and countless Acers planted from 1960.

There is a Japanese Garden, a Himalayan Garden with Mountain Tree Paeonies (p.suffruticosa) a Secret Garden with many rare species, a Rose Garden and a Catalpa Walk. The Victorian Kitchen Garden shelters a Vineyard planted in 2000 and a Palm Garden planted in 2002 with Washingtonia, Trachycarpus and Mexican Blue Palms plus Olive Trees and Cypresses and Cordylines.

Fact File

Opening Times:	For charity (NGS) Sunday 29th May 2pm - 6pm, and for RHS Saturday June 11th 2pm - 6pm. Groups by appointment only May - October.
Admission Rates:	Adults £4.00, Senior Citizens £4.00, Child £2.00, (NGS days only)
Groups Rates:	Minimum group size 25. (Guided tours by owner) Adults £5.00, Senior Citizens £5.00, Child £2.50
Facilities:	Teas, Plant Stall on 29th May. For groups by appointment.
Disabled Access:	Yes. Toilet and parking for disabled on site.
Tours/Events:	Wine tastings from our vineyard, dates to be announced.
Coach Parking:	Yes
Length of Visit:	1 - 2 Hours
Booking Contact:	Mr or Mrs Hamish Cathie Barton House, Barton-On-The-Heath, Moreton-In-Marsh, Glos, GL56 0PJ Telephone: 01608 674303 Fax: 01608 674365
Email:	None
Website:	None
Location:	Between Moreton-in-Marsh and Chipping Norton off A44 (Evesham - Oxford Road), Turn at sign "Barton 1 1/4".

Please quote this guide when booking

Batsford Arboretum & Wild Garden   Gloucestershire

Batsford Arboretum & Wild Garden - The Cotswolds Secret Garden and former home of the Mitford family.

One of the largest private collection of trees in Great Britain. See spring flowers as they cascade down the hillside. Many wild orchids and fritillaries adorn the arboretum. In autumn the many rare and unusual trees explode into their magnificent reds, golds and purples.

Follow the stream through pools and waterfalls to its source, make a wish with the giant Buddha. Find the Foo Dog hidden amongst the trees, then negotiate the waterfall without getting too wet. See if you can find Algernon and Clemantine on the lake, then rest awhile and view the deer in the Deer Park. Fifty acres of peace, traquillity - pure Cotswold magic!

Fact File

Opening Times:	10am - 5pm 1st February - 15th November.
	Week-ends only from 15th November - 1st February.
	Also open Boxing Day & New Years Day.
Admission Rates:	Adults £5.00, Senior Citizen £5.00, Child £1.00.
Groups Rates:	Minimum group size 12. Admission Rates less 10%
	Adults £5.00, Senior Citizens £5.00, Child £2.50
Facilities:	Visitor Centre, Shop, Plant Sales, Teas, Restaurant, Garden Centre and Falconry Centre.
Disabled Access:	Partial. Toilet and parking for disabled on site, wheelchairs on loan, booking necessary.
Tours/Events:	Tours by arrangement. Events to be arranged.
Coach Parking:	Yes new area.
Length of Visit:	2 Hours
Booking Contact:	Mr Chris Pilling
	Batsford Arboretum, Batsford Park, Moreton in Marsh, Glos GL56 9QB.
	Telephone: 01386 701441 Fax: 01386 701829
Email:	batsarb@batsfound.freeserve.co.uk
Website:	www.batsarb.co.uk
Location:	1 mile east of Moreton in Marsh on A44 road.

Please quote this guide when booking

Intensively planted, this 3-acre garden features excitingly planted herbaceous borders full of stunning plant and colour combinations.

Neatly clipped box and yew is found in knots, parterres and spiralling topiary. Water wends it way through small fountains, pools and ponds. A sub-tropical border, raised alpine troughs, a shadehouse, all provide further variety in this continually evolving garden, and add to the whole, a myriad of magically planted pots and containers.

Planted less than 10 years ago with a wide variety of trees, the seven-acre field opposite already boasts some sizeable specimens.

The imposing 16th century Tithe barn now houses a gallery of Contemporary Art, Craft and Design.

Fact File

Opening Times:	25th May - 31st August: Wednesday,Thursday & Friday. September - 28th October: Thursday & Friday only. 10am - 5pm.
Admission Rates:	Adults £5.00, Senior Citizen £4.50, Child Free.
Groups Rates:	Minimum group size 20 Adults £4.50, Senior Citizen £4.00, Child Free.
Facilities:	Gallery of Contemporary Art, Craft, Design in the Tithe Barn, Teas & Light Meals until mid September. Plants for sale.
Disabled Access:	There is limited access for wheelchairs: 70%
Tours/Events:	Please see website for current activities.
Coach Parking:	Yes
Length of Visit:	1 1/2 hours
Booking Contact:	Monique B Paice Bourton House, Bourton-On-The-Hill, Moreton-in-Marsh, Glos, GL56 9AE Tel: 01386 700121 Fax: 01386 701081
Email:	cd@bourtonhouse.com
Website:	www.bourtonhouse.com
Location:	2 miles west of Moreton-in Marsh on the A44.

Please quote this guide when booking

Hidcote Manor Garden

Hidcote Manor Garden is one of Englands's great Arts and Craft gardens. Created by the American horticulturist Major Lawrence Johnston in 1907, Hidcote is famous for its rare trees and shrubs, outstanding herbaceous borders and unusual plants from all over the world.

The garden is divided by tall hedges and walls to create a series of outdoor 'rooms' each with its own special and unique character. From the formal splendour of the White Garden and Bathing Pool to the informality and beauty of the Old Garden, visitors are assured of a surprise around every corner.

The numerous outdoor rooms reach their height at different times of the year, making a visit to Hidcote Manor Garden enjoyable whatever the season.

Fact File

Opening Times: 19 March - 30 October: Monday, Tuesday, Wednesday, Saturday & Sunday 10.30am - 6pm (last admission 5pm). From October last admission 4pm.

Admission Rates: Adults £6.60, Senior Citizen £6.60, Child £3.30

Groups Rates: Minimum group size: 15
Adults £5.90, Senior Citizen £5.90, Child £2.65 (National Trust members free)

Facilities: Shop, Plant Sales, Teas & Restaurant.

Disabled Access: Partial. Toilet and parking for disabled on site. Wheelchairs on loan.

Tours/Events: Please contact the property for a list of special events.

Coach Parking: Yes. Groups must book in advanced.

Length of Visit: 2 hours

Booking Contact: Lisa Edinborough,
Hidcote Manor Garden, Hidcote Bartrim, Chipping Campden, Gloucestershire, GL55 6LR
Telephone: 01386 438333   Fax: 01386 438817

Email: hidcote@nationaltrust.org.uk

Website: www. nationaltrust.org.uk/hidcote

Location: 4 miles north east of Chipping Campden; 8 miles south of Stratford Upon Avon & signposted from B4632 Stratford/Broadway road, close to the village of Mickleton.

Please quote this guide when booking

Kiftsgate Court Garden   Gloucestershire

Kiftsgate is a glorious garden to visit throughout the seasons with spectacular views to the Malvern Hills and beyond. Three generations of women gardeners have designed, planted and sustained this garden.

The upper gardens around the house are planted to give harmonious colour schemes, whilst the sheltered lower gardens recreate the atmosphere of warmer countries. The latest addition is a modern water garden which provides an oasis of tranquillity and contrast to the exuberance of the flower gardens.

On open days plants grown from the garden are for sale. A wide and interesting selection are always available. The tearoom in the house offers delicious home-made cream teas and light lunches in June and July.

"Winner of the HHA/Christies Garden of the Year award 2003"

Fact File

Opening Times: April, May, August, September - Wednesday, Thursday & Sunday 2pm - 6pm.
June & July - Monday, Wednesday, Thursday, Saturday & Sunday 12noon - 6pm.

Admission Rates: Adults £5.00, Senior Citizen £5.00, Child £1.50

Groups Rates: Coaches by appointment, 20 adults and more £4.50 per person

Facilities: Plants for Sale, Tea Room.

Disabled Access: No

Tours/Events: None

Coach Parking: Yes.

Length of Visit: 1 1/2 hours

Booking Contact: Mrs Anne Chambers
Kiftsgate Court Garden, Chipping Campden, Gloucestershire, GL55 6LN
Telephone: 01386 438777   Fax: 01386 438777

Email: kiftsgte@aol.com

Website: www.Kiftsgate.co.uk

Location: 3 miles north east of Chipping Campden. Follow signs towards Mickleton, then follow brown tourist signs to Kiftsgate Court Gardens.

Please quote this guide when booking

Lydney Park Spring Gardens   Gloucestershire

A place of tranquil beauty amidst fine formal gardens, Lydney Park is home to Viscount Bledisloe. Both Tolkein (1928/29) and the Dutch Royal Family (1939/40) stayed at Lydney Park which is steeped in history from Iron Age to the present day. In early season, the visitor to Lydney Park drives between a resplendent display of daffodils and narcissi, and beyond the car park are the Spring Gardens, a secret wooded valley with lakes, providing a profusion of Rhododendrons, Azaleas and other flowering shrubs. Discover an important Roman Temple Site and the site of a Normal Castle. Picnic in the Deer Park amongst some magnificent trees, and visit our museums, which includes a New Zealand Museum. Home-made teas in dining room of House. Dogs welcome on leads.

Fact File

Opening Times:	20th March - 5th June, Sun, Wed & Bank Hol Mons. 2nd - 8th May & 30th May - 5th June Daily.
Admission Rates:	Adults £4.00 (Wed £3.00) Senior Citizen £4.00, Child 50p
Groups Rate:	Minimum group size: 25 - Phone for group rates.
Facilities:	Gift Shop, Plant Sales, Teas.
Disabled Access:	Partial. Parking for disabled on site.
Tours/Events:	None
Coach Parking:	Yes
Length of Visit:	1 - 2 hours
Booking Contact:	Sally James
	Lydney Park Gardens, Lydney Park, Estate Office, Old Park, Lydney, Gloucestershire, GL15 6BU.
	Telephone: 01594 842844 Fax: 01594 842027
Email:	lydneypark@agriplus,net
Website:	None
Location:	Situated off A48 between Chepstow and Gloucester.

Please quote this guide when booking

The Matara Gardens Gloucestershire

Matara is a new and emerging meditative garden alive with inspiration from around the world. We invite you to explore and discover our labyrinths, medicine wheel, ponds, sculptures and walled ornamental vegetable garden. We are developing an Eastern woodland walk and wildflower meadow.

Matara is a unique spiritual garden dedicated to the full expression of the human spirit. Based on ecologically sound principles, the grounds offer the chance to re-establish relationships with the natural world. Come and wander through a range of peaceful areas, all set within the great beauty of our 28-acre parkland.

Afterwards, relax and enjoy teas and cake in the Matara Centre. We look forward to your visit and hope you will come back many times.

Fact File

Opening Times:	May - September (or by appointment) 1pm - 5pm Wednesdays, Fridays & Sundays.
Admission Rates:	Adults £3.00, Senior Citizen £3.00, Child under 16 free.
Group Rates:	Minimum group size: 20
	Adults £2.50, Senior Citizen £2.50, Child under 16 free.
Facilities:	Teas and Cakes.
Disabled Access:	Partial. Toilet and parking for disabled on site.
Tours/Events:	None
Coach Parking:	Yes (Pre-booked only)
Length of Visit:	3 hours
Booking Contact:	Matara Garden
	Kingscote Park (nr Tetbury), Kingscote, Gloucestershire, GL8 8YA.
	Telephone: 01453 860084 Fax: 01453 861080
Email:	info@matara.co.uk
Website:	www.matara.co.uk
Location:	On A4135 towards Dursley, at Hunters Hall Inn turn right into Kingscote village. Enter park at 1st gate on the right.

Please quote this guide when booking

Mill Dene Garden   Gloucestershire

Mill Dene Garden surrounds an old Cotswold stone water-mill dating back to Norman times and is set in its own steeply sided valley. The garden has been designed and planted by the owner, Wendy Dare for all season interest.

The garden seems to have evolved naturally in typical 'English country garden' relaxed style. From the tranquil mill-pond, stream and grotto at the bottom of the garden (with frost pocket and bog garden) steep terraces rise along terraces with a trompe l'oeil to tease the eye. A new bed of highly scented roses with lavender at their feet look good in June/July and September. On the next level is the Cricket lawn with high Summer borders and at the very top of the garden backed by the village Church and with views over the Cotswolds hills, are the Fantasy Fruit garden and the Potager with medicinal and culinary plants.

A garden made from a field not long ago offers challenges of a north facing and shady site cleverly overcome.

Fact File

Opening Times: 5th April - 28th October, Tuesday to Friday, 10am - 5.30pm, Saturday, Sunday and Mondays by appointment only.

Admission Rates: Adults £4.50, Senior Citizen £4.00, Child under 15 £1.00

Groups Rates: Minimum group size: 20
£4.00 for groups of 20 or more. (Coaches by appointment)

Facilities: Tea, Coffee, Home made cakes, light lunches for groups of under 15.

Disabled Access: Partial. Parking for disabled on site by arrangement.

Tours/Events: Introductory talk - 10 to 15 mins £25.00. Guided tour by owner £100.00.

Coach Parking: Nearby, map provided. (Limited parking for 10 cars.)

Length of Visit: 1 1/2 hours

Booking Contact: Mrs Wendy Dare.
Mill Dene, Blockley, Moreton-in-Marsh, Gloucestershire, GL56 9HU.
Telephone : 01386 700457 Fax: 01386 700526

Email: info@milldene.co.uk

Website: www.milldenegarden.co.uk

Location: Take the Blockley turn off the A44 at Bourton on the Hill only.
Coaches follow brown signs, stop at 1st left turn behind village gates by School Lane, and unload, then park in the village sports ground.

Please quote this guide when booking

59

This lovely timeless English Garden, which commands spectacular views over the Golden Valley has most of the features one would expect a garden started in the 17th century. There are extensive yew hedges and a notable yew walk dividing the walled garden, the york stone terrace, the Lutyens Loggia overhung with Wisteria, and a good specimen of magnolia sulangiana. The south lawn supports splendid grass steps and a fine Mulberry (probably planted when the original house was built in 1620). West of the house the ground descends a series of grasses, terraces and shrubberies. Within the walled garden are two good herbaceous borders, amongst the longest in the country. The walls are planted with climbing and rambler roses and there is a rose pergola dividing the border. A rill with a fountain and the stone summer-house were added as a feature to mark the new Millennium. More recently a circular parterre has been established with tulips, alliums, hebes and lavender. There are many fine specimen trees and the spring show of blossom and bulbs is notable.

Fact File

Opening Times:	10am - 5pm, Tuesday, Wednesday & Thursday, 1st April - 30th September.
Admission Rates:	Adults £3.50, Senior Citizen £3.50, Child Free
Group Rates:	Minimum group size: 20
	Adults £3.15, Senior Citizen £3.15, Child Free
Facilities:	Nurseries Adjacent.
Disabled Access:	Yes. Parking for disabled on site.
Tours/Events:	None.
Coach Parking:	Yes
Length of Visit:	1 1/2 hours
Booking Contact:	Major M.T.N.H. Wills
	Misarden Park, Miserden, Stroud, Glos, GL6 7JA
	Telephone 01285 821303 Fax: 01285 821530
Email:	estate.office@miserdenestate.co.uk
Website:	None
Location:	Follow signs to Miserden from A417 or from B4070.

Please quote this guide when booking

Historic formal hillside garden, Stuart period. The Tudor Manor house (1450-1616), garden and outbuildings lie in a picturesque wooded setting under the Cotswold hills.

The terraced garden is a rare survival of an early formal garden on a manorial scale, re-ordered in 1723, with magnificent yew topiary, old roses and box parterres. After being uninhabited for over 100 years, it was restored sympathetically in 'Old English' style by Norman Jewson in 1926.

Fact File

Opening Times: 1st April to 30th September, Tuesdays to Sundays and Bank Holiday Mondays, Gardens and Restaurant 10.30 - 5.00pm.

Admission Rates: Adults £4.80, Senior Citizen £4.80, Child £2.00

Groups Rates: Minimum group size: 15
Adults £4.50, Senior Citizen £4.50, Child £2.00

Facilities: Restaurant, Lunches and Teas.

Disabled Access: No. Parking for disabled on site.

Tours/Events: None.

Coach Parking: Yes.

Length of Visit: 1 1/2 - 2 hours

Booking Contact: Owlpen Estate Office
Owlpen Manor, Uley, Dursley, Gloucestershire, GL11 5BZ
Telephone: 01453 860261   Fax: 01453 860819

Email: sales@owlpen.com

Website: www.owlpen.com

Location: 1/2 mile east off B4066 at village green in Uley, between Dursley and Stroud.

Please quote this guide when booking

Painswick Rococo Garden   Gloucestershire

Painswick Rococo Garden is a fascinating insight into 18th century English garden design. The only complete Rococo garden in England, it dates from a brief period (1720-1760) when English gardens where changing from the formal to the informal. These Rococo gardens combined formal vists with winding woodland walks and more natural planting. However Rococo gardens were so much more, their creators showed off their wealth and included features that were both flamboyant and frivolous. The gardens featured buildings of unusual architectural styles, to be used as both eye catchers and view points. These gardens became regency playrooms, an extension of the house to be enjoyed by the owner and his guests.

We are restoring the garden back to how it was shown in a painting dated 1748. We have contemporary buidings, woodland walks, herbaceous borders, and a large kitchen garden all hidden away in a charming Cotswold valley with splendid views of the surrounding countryside.

Fact File

Opening Times:	10th January - 31st October. Daily 11am - 5pm.
Admission Rates:	Adults £4.00, Senior Citizen £3.50, Child £2.00
Groups Rates:	Minimum group size: 20 (includes free introductory talk)
	Adults £3.50, Senior Citizen £3.50
Facilities:	Visitor Centre, Shop, Plant Sales, Teas, Restaurant.
Disabled Access:	No. Toilet for disabled on site.
Tours/Events:	None.
Coach Parking:	Yes.
Length of Visit:	2 hours
Booking Contact:	Paul Moir
	Painswick Rococo Garden, Gloucestershire, GL6 6TH
	Telephone: 01452 813204 Fax: 01452 814888
Email:	prm@rococogarden.co.uk
Website:	www.rococogarden.co.uk
Location:	1/2 mile outside Painswick on B4073

Please quote this guide when booking

Rodmarton Manor

Gloucestershire

Rodmarton Manor is the supreme example of the Cotswold Arts and Crafts Movement. The garden was laid out as the house was being built (1909-1929) as a series of outdoor rooms covering about 8 acres. Each garden room has a different character and is bounded by either walls or hedges. One "garden room" has 26 separate beds with a wide variety of planting dominated by yellow shrubs and roses. There is a collection of stone troughs with alpines as well a rockery with bigger alpines. Topiary is a feature of the garden with extensive yew, box beech and holly hedges and clipped features including some new topiary. The herbaceous borders are magnificent from May but peaking late June but with plenty flowering into September. Many different types of roses flourish in the garden including old fashioned well-scented ones. There is a walled Kitchen Garden which has other plants besides vegetables including trained apples and pears. There is a big snowdrop collection. Most people who visit Rodmarton see the house which has specially made furniture as well as seeing the garden.

Fact File

Opening Times: 13th, 17th, 20th February from 1.30pm, (Garden only).
Wednesdays, Saturdays, Bank Holidays 2nd May - 17th September 2pm - 5pm.
Private coach bookings at other times.

Admission Rates: House and Garden £7.00 (5-15yrs £3.50). Garden only £4.00 (5 - 15yrs £1.00)

Facilities: Teas

Disabled Access: Yes. Most of garden and ground floor of house.

Coach Parking: Yes

Length of Visit: 2 hours for house and garden

Booking Contact: Simon Biddulph,
Rodmarton Manor, Cirencester, GL7 6PF.
Telephone 01285 841253 Fax: 01285 841298

Email: simon.biddulph@farming.co.uk

Website: www.rodmarton-manor.co.uk

Location: Off A433 between Cirencester and Tetbury.
(no dogs)

Please quote this guide when booking

Sudeley Castle & Gardens — Gloucestershire

Surrounding Sudeley Castle are 14 acres of glorious, organically managed gardens. Designed almost as a continuation of the house they surround, a number of smaller individual gardens blend seamlessly together. Bold areas of planting such as those surrounding the 15th century Tithe Barn ruins contrast with intricate detail as seen in the Tudor Knot Garden. Topiary features strongly throughout and the famous Queens Garden, full of English roses, is furnished on two sides by magnificent double yew hedges planted in 1860. A Victorian Vegetable Garden works with the HDRA to help preserve rare and endangered vegetables. More recent additions include the East Garden, its arbour and beds planted with white wisterias, oriental clematis and tree peonies, and a newly landscaped pheasantry and wildfowl area.

Fact File

Opening Times: Gardens - Open daily 26th February - 30th October 2005, 10.30am - 5.30pm.
Castle Exhibitions - open 19th March - 30th October, 11am - 5.00pm.

Admission Rates: Please call for details or visit our website.

Group Rates: Group rates available.

Facilities: Visitor Centre, Shop, Plant Sales, Resaurant and Picnic Area.

Disabled Access: Limited - garden only. Toilet and Parking for disabled on site.

Tours/Events: Guided tours available - must be pre-booked. Special events programme, please call for details. (Information may be subject to change, please call or check website).

Coach Parking: Yes

Length of Visit: 3 hours

Booking Contact: Group Bookings
Sudeley Castle, Winchcombe, Cheltenham, Gloucestershire, GL54 5JD
Telephone: 01242 602308 Fax: 01242 602959

Email: marketing@sudeley.org.uk

Website: www.sudeleycastle.co.uk

Location: On B4632, 8 miles north east of Cheltenham.

Please quote this guide when booking

The gardens were laid out in the early 20th Century and this structure has been added to since then. The principle features are the lily pond, the sunken garden, the wilderness and the walled gardens.

Within the walled gardens behind the house are herbaceous borders that contain many unusual plants cleverly planted providing a spectacle from May to September. In front of the beautiful Cotswold Stone House are large expanses of lawn surrounded by mature trees. Views from the gardens are breathtaking.

The cosy atmosphere and size of the garden (8 acres) make it an ideal place to visit whether individually or as a group. Home-made teas are available and other refreshments can be arranged for groups. Access and parking are easy.

The garden was featured in *Country Living* and *Roots and Shoots* in 2003. A haven in the Cotswolds not to be missed.

Fact File

Opening Times:	Wednesdays, Saturdays and Bank Holidays - 30th April - 3rd September 2005.
Admission Rates:	Adults £3.50, Children under 16 free.
Group Rates:	Minimum group size: 20+
	Adults £3.00, Children under 16 free.
Facilities:	WC, Plant Sales, Pots and Garden Furniture for sale.
Disabled Access:	Yes.
Tours/Events:	Please call for details.
Coach Parking:	Yes
Length of Visit:	1 + hours
Booking Contact:	Simon Mitchell
	Trull House, Nr. Tetbury, Gloucestershire, GL8 8SQ.
	Telephone: 01285 841255
Email:	simonmitchell@btconnect.com
Website:	www.trullhouse.co.uk
Location:	3 miles east of Tetbury off A433. Follow signs.

Please quote this guide when booking

The Grade I listed gardens of Westonbirt School were designed by Robert Holford (1808-1892), best known as founder of the National Arboretum at Westonbirt. Both the School Gardens and the Arboretum were originally part of the same private estate, with Westonbirt House, now the main school building, at its heart.

The School Gardens include many notable specimen trees as well as extensive terraced 'pleasure grounds', Italianate walled gardens, water features, statuary, a grotto, a grass amphitheatre, and wooded walks to a lake.

Many visitors combine their visit to Westonbirt School Gardens with a trip to the nearby Arboretum and find it fascinating to spot the similarities and differences between the formal, highly architectural School Gardens and the Arboretum. NB The National Arboretum at Westonbirt is now owned and operated by the Forestry Commission and a separate entry charge is payable.

Fact File

Opening Times:	Thursday - Sunday only on 20th March - 10th April, 10th July - 3rd Sept., 22nd - 30th Oct.
Admission Rates:	Adults £3.50, Senior Citizen £3.50, Child £2.00 (under 5s free).
Groups Rates:	Group Rates on application/subject to negotiation and discussion of exact requirements e.g. whether guide required, refreshments etc.
Facilities:	Refreshments on sale from ticket office (cold drinks, confectionery)
Disabled Access:	Yes. Parking for disabled on site.
Tours/Events:	Tours by arrangement.
Coach Parking:	Yes
Length of Visit:	Allow 1 1/2 - 2 Hours
Booking Contact:	Jack Doyle Westonbirt School, Tetbury, Gloucestershire, GL8 8QG Telephone: 01666 881338 Fax: 01666 880364
Email:	doyle@westonbirt.gloucs.sch.uk
Website:	www.westonbirt.gloucs.sch.uk
Location:	On A433, 3 miles SW of Tetbury, opposite Westonbirt Arboretum which is clearly marked by brown tourist information signs form all directions.

Please quote this guide when booking

Westonbirt, The National Arboretum Gloucestershire

Westonbirt is a wonderful world of trees and is beautiful at any time of year. Set in 600 acres of glorious Cotswold countryside, it has 17 miles of paths along which to stroll and over 18,000 numbered trees, including 100 champions - the oldest, largest, tallest of that species in the country.

In spring it is ablaze with colour from rhododendrons, azaleas, magnolias and bluebells, but is more famous for its autumn colour, when it seems almost every tree turns a brilliant red, orange or gold. Summer brings cool leafy glades where butterflies and bees busily collect nectar, and an exciting events programme including The Festival of Wood. Add to this a restaurant, shop and plant centre and you have a perfect day out.

Fact File

Opening Times: 10am - 8pm or dusk if earlier.

Admission Rates: Adults from £5.00, Senior Citizens from £4.00, Child £1.00. Please see website for confirmation at time of visit.

Group Rates: Group rates available, please telephone for details.

Facilities: Shop, Plant Sales, Cafe, Restaurant.

Disabled Access: Yes. Toilet and parking for disabled on site. Wheelchairs on loan, booking necessary.

Tours/Events: Festival of Wood - August, Enchanted Wood - December, Summer Concerts

Coach Parking: Yes

Length of Visit: 2 - 3 hours

Booking Contact: Helen Daniels
Westonbirt Arboretum, Tetbury, Gloucestershire, GL8 8QS.
Telephone: 01666 880220 Fax: 01666 880559

Email: westonbirt@forestry.gsi.gov.uk

Website: www.forestry.gov.uk/westonbirt

Location: 15 mins north east of junction 18 M4.

Please quote this guide when booking

Exbury Gardens & Steam Railway   Hampshire

Natural beauty is in abundance at Exbury Gardens, a 200 - acre woodland garden on the east bank of the Beaulieu river. Created by Lionel de Rothschild in the 1920's the Gardens are a stunning vision of his inspiration. The spring displays of rhododendrons, azaleas, camellias and magnolias are world famous. The daffodil meadow, rock garden, exotic garden and herbaceous and grasses garden, ponds and cascades ensure year round interest. Exbury is a previous winner of Christie's Garden of the Year.

The Exbury Gardens Railway proves very popular with visitors. Why not 'let the train take the strain' on a 1 1/4 mile journey over a bridge, through a tunnel, across a pond in the Summer Lane Garden planted with bulbs, herbaceous perennials and grasses? Then travel along the top of the rock garden and across a viaduct into the American Garden.

New for 2005: Exbury Museum, new catering facilities; special events to mark the 50th Anniversary of the gardens opening to the public.

Fact File

Opening Times: 26th February - 6th November 10am - 5.30pm

Admission Rates: (H/S-L/S) Adult £7.00/£5.00, Senior Citizen £6.50/£4.50, Child (3-15) £1.50/£1.00 under 3's Free, Family £17.00/£12.00, (2 Adults & 3 Children 3-15). Railway £3.00/£2.50 extra.

Groups Rates: Minimum group size: 15 - Adults £6.50/£4.50.

Facilities: Gift Shop, Plant Sales, Teas, Restaurant, Buggy Tours.

Disabled Access: Yes. Toilet and parking for disabled on site. Wheelchairs on loan. Accessible carriages on train.

Tours/Events: Please call for info on guided tours and 'Meet & Greets' by arrangement on 023 80 891203. Please call for details of special events, or visit our website.

Coach Parking: Yes

Length of Visit: 2 - 3 hours

Booking Contact: Barbara King
Exbury Gardens, Estate Office, Exbury, Southampton, Hants SO45 1AZ.
Telephone: 023 80 891203 Fax: 023 80 899940

Email: nigel.philpott@exbury.co.uk

Website: www.exbury.co.uk

Location: Junction 2 west of M27, just follow A326 to Fawley, off B3054, 3 miles Beaulieu.

Please quote this guide when booking

Hinton Ampner Garden   Hampshire

I have learned during the past years what above all I want from a garden: this is 'tranquillity'. So said Ralph Dutton, 8th and last Lord Sherborne, of his garden at Hinton Ampner. In the 1930's he created one of the great gardens of the 20th century, a masterpiece of design based upon the bones of a Victorian garden, in which he united a formal layout with varied and informal planting in pastel shades. It is a garden of all year round interest with scented plants and magnificent vistas over the park and surrounding countryside.

The garden forms the link between the woodland and parkland planting and the house, which he remodelled into a small neo-Georgian manor house and which contains his very fine collection of paintings and furniture. It is all set within the rolling Hampshire landscape that he loved and understood so well.

Fact File

Opening Times: Garden Open: Sun 20 March. Then 26th March - 28th September 12pm- 5pm
(Daily **except** Thursday & Friday).
House Open: 29th March - 28th September 1.30pm - 5pm
Tuesday & Wednesday only (Saturday & Sunday August only).

Admission Rates: Garden - £5.00, House & Garden - £6.00, Child (5-16) 1/2 price.

Group Rates: Minimum group size: 15 - must be pre-booked.
House & Garden £5.30,

Facilities: Tea Room

Disabled Access: Yes. Toilet and Parking for disabled on site. Wheelchairs on loan.

Tours/Events: Monthly 'Meet the Gardener' walks and occasional demonstrations.

Coach Parking: Yes but must be pre booked.

Length of Visit: 2 hours

Booking Contact: Nick Brooks
Hinton Ampner Garden, Bramdean, nr Alresford, Hampshire, SO24 0LA.
Telephone: 01962 771305 Fax: 01962 793101

Email: hintonampner@nationaltrust.org.uk

Website: www.nationaltrust.org.uk

Location: On A272 mid way between Winchester and Petersfield.

Please quote this guide when booking

Mottisfont Abbey and Garden

Hampshire

Mottisfont boasts thirty acres of landscaped grounds with sweeping lawns and magnificent trees, set amidst glorious countryside along the River Test.

The extensive gardens were remodelled gradually during the 20th century. Norah Lindsay designed a parterre, Geofrey Jellicoe redesigned the north front with an avenue of pollarded limes and an octagon of yews, all combine to provide interest throughout the seasons. Graham Stuart Thomas designed the walled garden in 1972, with beds divided by attractive box hedges, to contain the NATIONAL COLLECTION of OLD FASHIONED ROSES, with over 300 varieties. It is at its best in mid June, but has plenty to interest visitors later in summer and autumn.

The twelfth century Augustine priory is now a house of some note, containing delightful rooms such as the drawing room decorated by Rex Whistler in "trompe l'oeil" fantasy style. It also houses an interesting collection of 19th and early 20th century pictures donated by painter Derek Hill.

Fact File

Opening Times: Please telephone the information line for details 01794 341220.
Admission Rates: Adults £7.00, Senior Citizen £7.00, Child, £3.50, Family £17.50
Group Rates: Minimum group size: 15
                        Group rate £6.00 per adult.
Facilities: Visitor Centre, Shop, Plant Sales, Teas, Kitchen Cafe.
Disabled Access: Yes. Toilet and Parking for disabled on site. Wheelchairs on loan.
Tours/Events: See Mottisfont event brochure.
Coach Parking: Yes
Length of Visit: 2 hours
Booking Contact   Mottisfont Abbey, Mottisfont, Nr Romsey, Hampshire, SO51 0LP
                        Telephone 01794 344018 Fax: 01794 341429
Email: mottisfontabbey@nationaltrust.org
Website: www.nationaltrust,org
Location: Signposted off A3057, Romsey to Stockbridge road, 4 miles north of Romsey.

Please quote this guide when booking

Sir Harold Hillier Gardens   Hampshire

Sir Harold Hillier Gardens is one of the most important modern plant collections in the world. Established in 1953 by the distinguished plantsman Sir Harold Hillier, the magnificent collection of over 42,000 plants from temperate regions around the world grows in a variety of superb themed landscaped set over 180-acres if rolling Hampshire countryside.

Open throughout the year, every part of the gardens offers beauty, inspiration and discovery whatever the season and includes 11 National Plant Collections, over 250 Champion Trees and the largest winter Garden in Europe.

A newly opened £3.5 million Visitor & Education Pavilion offers fine views of the collection and surrounding countryside and features; a stylish licensed restaurant for home-cooked meals, light refreshments and afternoon teas; open-air terrace; gift shop; and interpretation area explaining the role and history of the Gardens. Entry to the Pavilion is free of charge with Group bookings welcome by prior arrangement.

Fact File

Opening Times:	Daily: 10.30am - 6pm or dusk if earlier. Open all year except Christmas Day and Boxing Day.
Admission Rates:	Adults £7.00, Concession £6.00, Senior Citizen £6.00, Child under 16 yrs free.
Groups Rates:	Minimum group size 10 Adults £5.50, Senior Citizen £5.50.
Facilities:	New £3.5 million Visitor & Education Pavilion, Open-air terrace and restaurant, Gift Shop, Plant Centre.
Disabled Access:	Yes. Toilet and parking for disabled on site. Wheelchairs on loan, booking advised, Mobility Scooters for hire.
Tours/Events:	Pre-booked guided tour with Curator, Botanist, Head Gardener and Horticultural staff available by arrangement. Please telephone for details about Special Events.
Coach Parking:	Yes (Free)
Length of Visit:	2 - 4 hours
Booking Contact:	Group Bookings. Sir Harold Hillier Gardens, Jermyns Lane, Romsey, Hampshire, SO51 0QA Telephone: 01794 368787 Fax: 01794 368027
Email:	info@hilliergardens.org.uk **Website:** www.hilliergardens.org.uk
Location:	The Gardens are situated, 3 miles north-east of Romsey. M3/M27 (West) to Romsey town centre. At Romsey follow brown heritage signs to the Hillier Gardens off the A3090. Alternatively, the Gardens can be approached from the A3057 Andover direction.

Please quote this guide when booking

West Green House Gardens   Hampshire

Nestling in a woodland corner of Hampshire is this ravishingly attractive 1720's manor house, where busts of gods, emperors and dukes look down from the walls onto two major gardens. The inner gardens, enclosed by eighteenth century walls, are all devoted to parterres. One is filled with water lilles, another of classical design with box topiary and a third enacts the whimsy of *Alice in Wonderland* with the story's characters in ivy and box topiary surrounded by roses of red and white. The main walled garden is planted in subtle hues of mauve, plum and blue, contained in beds that have been faithfully restored to their original outlines. A decorative potager is centred around berry-filled fruit cages where herbs, flowers and unusual vegetables are designed into colourful patterns. All this is surrounded by a second garden, a remarkable new-classical park studded with follies, birdcages and monuments. In 2004 a Paradise Walk garden was opened.

West Green House was the first garden to have a whole 'Gardeners World' programme dedicated to itself.

Fact File

Opening Times:	Open 1st April to 31st August, Thursday - Sunday and Bank Holiday Mondays. September, Saturday and Sunday 11am - 4.30pm.
Admission Rates:	Adults £5.00.
Group Rates:	Groups by arangement please telephone for details.
Facilities:	Tea/Coffee Shop serving light lunches, Garden Shop.
Disabled Access:	Yes. Toilet and parking for disabled on site.
Tours/Events:	Plant Fair at Easter, Music Season - please telephone for details.
Coach Parking:	Yes
Length of Visit:	2 hours approximately.
Booking Contact:	West Green House, Thackhams Lane, West Green, Hartley Wintney, Hants RG27 8JB Telephone: 01252 845582 Fax: 01252 844611
Email:	None
Website:	westgreenhousegarden.com.uk
Location:	10 miles north east of Basingstoke, 1 mile west of Hartley Wintney, 1 mile north of A30.

Please quote this guide when booking

Hergest Croft Gardens

Herefordshire

From Spring bulbs to Autumn colour, this is a garden for all seasons. With over 60 champion trees and shrubs, the Gardens are recognised as "one of the best collections of plants held in private ownership", holding National Collections of Maples, Birches and Zelkovas. Rhododendrons and Azaleas are spectacular in Spring, and the large kitchen garden with the long double herbaceous borders, Rose Garden and Spring Borders are always attractive. Autumn colours are superb.

Teas with local home-made food are available in the old dining-room. Rare and unusual plants are for sale, the majority grown in the garden, and there is a shop selling a wide range of gifts.

There are special entry rates for pre-booked groups of 20 or more people.

Fact File

Opening Times: Weekends in March, March 25th to October 30th 12-30pm - 5.30pm.
May to June 12.00pm - 6.00pm.

Admission Rates: Adults £5.00, Senior Citizen £5.00, Child Free

Group Rates: Minimum group size: 20 +
Adults £4.00, Senior Citizen £4.00, Child Free

Facilities: Shop, Plant Sales, Light Lunches and Teas.

Disabled Access: Yes. but limited to certain areas. Toilet and parking for disabled on site.
Wheelchair on loan, booking necessary.

Tours/Events: Pre booked guided tours @ £6.00 (including entrace) Monday 2nd May Flower Fair,
Sunday 16th October Plant Fair.

Coach Parking: Yes

Length of Visit: 2 + Hours

Booking Contact: Melanie Lloyd
Hergest Croft Gardens, Kington, Herefordshire, HR5 3EG
Telephone: 01544 230160 Fax: 01544 232031

Email: gardens@hergest.co.uk

Website: www.hergest.co.uk

Location: Follow brown tourist signs off the A44 Rhayader.

Please quote this guide when booking

The Gardens at Hatfield House date from the early 17th century when Robert Cecil, 1st Earl of Salisbury, employed John Tradescant the Elder to plant and lay them out around his new home. Tradescant was sent to Europe where he found and brought back trees, bulbs, plants and fruit trees, which had never previously been grown in England.

These beautifully designed gardens included orchards, elaborate fountains, scented plants, water parterres, terraces, herb gardens and a foot maze. Following the fashion for landscape gardening and some neglect in the 18th century, restoration of these gardens started in earnest in Victorian times. The gardens to the west of the house, which include the Herb, Knot and Wilderness areas, can be seen when the house is open. However, all 42 acres, including the Kitchen Garden and the formal parterres to the East of the house leading down to the lake, are open on Mondays (except bank holidays).

Fact File

Opening Times: Easter Saturday - end September, (except Thursdays & Fridays), 11am - 5.30pm.

Admission Rates: Adults £4.50, Senior Citizen £4.50, Child £3.50 (Monday £6.50 - no concessions).

Facilities: Tea Room, Restaurant, Gift Shop, Kiosk, Park Nature Trails.

Disabled Access: Yes. Toilet and parking for disabled on site.

Tours/Events: Flower Festival 10-12th June.
Hatfield Country Show 19th - 21st August

Coach Parking: Yes

Length of Visit: 2 1/2 hours

Booking Contact: House Office
Hatfield House, Hatfield, Hertfordshire. AL9 5NQ
Telephone: 01707 287010 Fax: 01707 287033

Email: visitors@hatfield-house.co.uk

Website: www.hatfield-house.co.uk

Location: 21 miles north of London. M25 junction 23, seven miles. A1(M) junction 4 two miles.
Signed of A414 and A1000. Opposite Hatfield Rail Station.

Please quote this guide when booking

Knebworth House, Gardens and Park   Hertfordshire

Much of the layout of the present 25 acres of Gardens at Knebworth House date from Edwin Lutyens' design in the early 1900s. There are 18 different 'rooms' to be seen including a Rose Garden with lily ponds and herbaceous borders , a Sunken Lawn, Green and Gold Gardens, a Brick Garden with blue and silver plantings and a Pergola. A Pets Cemetry, Maze and Ponds can be also seen.

The Walled Garden contains culinary herbs and vegetables, whilst the Gertrude Jekyll Herb Garden designed in 1907, was not laid out until 1982. The Wilderness and Woodland Walk which is a carpet of daffodils in spring followed by blue alkanet, foxgloves and other wild flowers now has the added attraction of the new dinosaur trail.

Fact File

Opening Times:	Daily 26th Mar - 10th April, 28th May - 5th June, 1st July - 4th Sept
	Weekends & Bank Holidays only, 19-20 Mar, 16 Apr - 22 May, 11-26 June, 11-25 Sept
Admission Rates:	Adults £6.50, Senior Citizens £6.50, Child £6.50 (All Excluding House).
Group Rates:	Minimum group size: 20
	Adults £5.60, Senior Citizens £5.60, Child £5.60 (All Excluding House).
Facilities:	Car & Coach Parking, WC, Shop, Tearoom, Picnic Area.
Disabled Access:	Partial. Toilet and parking for disabled on site, Wheelchairs available.
Tours/Events:	21st-22nd May, Herefordshire Garden Show.
Coach Parking:	Yes
Length of Visit:	3 hours
Booking Contact:	Knebworth House Gardens and Park, Knebworth, Hertfordshire, SG3 6PY
	Telephone: 01438 8122661 Fax: 01438 811908
Email:	info@knebworthouse.com
Website:	www.knebworthhouse.com
Location:	30 miles north of central London, direct access from Junction 7 of the A1M.

Please quote this guide when booking

The terraces have been restored to their Victorian layout and are once again planted in seasonally changing Victorian bedding. The walled fruit and flower garden has been restored. Features include a variety of Victorian trained fruit trees, expansive cut flower borders and rose and fruit arches. Herbaceous borders are planted with sub tropical and unusual species, very fashionable at the time of Queen Victoria.

See pleasure grounds containing mature specimens of unusual trees, many of which were some of the first introductions into Britain. The garden adjoining the Swiss Cottage was built for Victoria and Albert's children to learn the domestic skills of gardening. Vegetables and fruit were grown which were sold to Prince Albert, at commercial rates, providing the children with a practical exercise in market gardening.

The Ring Walk has been restored and takes in historic features like the mount, pond and the restored ice-house.

Fact File

Opening Times:	24th March - 31st October, 10am - 6pm daily (to 4pm in Oct, closed Fri/Sat).
Admission Rates:	House & Grounds, (Grounds) Adult £8.95 (£5.30) Senior Citizen £6.70 (£4.00), Child £4.50 (£2.70).
Group Rates:	Minimum group size: 11 House & Grounds Adult £7.60, Senior Citizen £5.70, Child £3.83.
Facilities:	Gift Shop, Plant Sales, Teas, Restaurant, Baby Changing, Toilets.
Disabled Access:	Partial. Toilet and parking for disabled on site. Wheelchair on loan.
Tours/Events:	None
Coach Parking:	Yes
Length of Visit:	3 hours
Booking Contact:	Osborne House, York Avenue, East Cowes, Isle of Wight, PO32 6JY Telephone: 01983 200022 Fax: 01983 281380
Email:	None
Website:	www.english-heritage.org.uk
Location:	1 mile south east of East Cowes (map196i ref SZ516948). Buses - Southern Vectis Services 4 Ryde - East Cowes and 5 Newport - East Cowes.

Please quote this guide when booking

Originally an offshot of Hilliers Nursery, Ventnor Botanic Garden is devoted to exotic plants. It is not strictly a *botanic* garden, but it has a remarkable collection. Many of the plants - perhaps most - are from the southern hemisphere but flourish in the unique microclimate of the 'Undercliff': widdringtonias from Zimbabwe and Tasmanian olearias, for instance, as well as astelias, *Sophora microphylla* and *Griselinia lucinda* from New Zealand. *Geranium maderense* has naturalised on the sunny slopes and so has an amazing colony of 4m *Echium pininana*. Elsewhere are such Mediterranean natives as acanthus, cistus and *Coronilla valentina*, and a remarkable area called the Palm Garden, where stately foliage plants like yuccas, cordylines, phoriums and beschornerias are underplanted with watsonias, cannas and kniphofias. Almost destroyed by the gales of 1987 and 1990, the collection were rapidly re-made and the garden looks wonderfully vigorous again. 2001 saw some extensive re-landscaping of the Mediterranean Garden. The energetic head gardener has a splendid eye for planting. A magnificent Visitor Centre opened recently: It offers the venue for exhibitions, conferences and a programme of events as well as a restaurant for visitors. The nursery sells some very interesting and often tender plants.

Fact File

Opening Times: Gardens all year round, dawn - dusk. Show-house & Plant Sales: 10am - 5pm daily, March - October, 10am - 4pm weekends, November - February. Visitor Centre: 10am - 5pm daily, March - October. 10am - 4pm except Monday + Friday, November - February.

Admission Rates: Gardens, Visitor Centre and Plant Sales - free of charge. Showhouse - small admission. Car parking charges apply.

Facilities: Visitor Centre, 'Green House' Exhibition, Plant Sales, Gift shop, Cafe. Conference & Function Facilities.

Disabled Access: Yes. Toilet and Parking for disabled on site. Wheelchairs on loan.

Tours/Events: Please telephone for details.

Coach Parking: Yes.

Length of Visit: 2 - 3 hours

Booking Contact: Alison Ellsbury
Ventnor Botanic Garden, Undercliff Drive, Ventnor, Isle of Wight, PO38 1UL
Telephone: 01983 855397 Fax: 01983 856756

Email: alison.ellsbury@iow.gov.uk

Website: www.botanic.co.uk

Location: Situated between Ventnor and St Lawrence on the A3055 coastal road.

Please quote this guide when booking

Bedgebury Pinetum   Kent

Bedgebury Pinetum, situated in the High Weald of Kent, currently has the world's largest collection of temperate conifers on one site in the world. The diversity of colour and form of the conifers is amazing and there are 91 rare or endangered species being cared for as part of Bedgebury's worldwide conservation effort.

The Pinetum is a haven of tranquillity and peace set in beautiful parkland with lakes, streams, rolling hills and wide avenues. Every season has its own charm: a fall of snow created a winter wonderland, there are carpets of bluebells flanked by magnificent rhododendrons and azaleas in spring, acres of wild flowers in summer, and shrubs and trees giving autumn colour, all set against the backdrop of the stunning conifers.

Fact File

Opening Times: 10am - 6pm Summer, 10am - 4pm Winter.
Admission Rates: Adults £4.00, Senior Citizens £3.50, Child £2.00, (under 4's free). Family (2+4) £10.00.
Groups Rates: Minimum group size 20+ less 10%, 40+ less 20%
Facilities: Visitor Centre, Shop, Teas and Light Snacks.
Disabled Access: Partial. Toilet and Parking for disabled on site.
Tours/Events: Please telephone for details of events, list available from shop.
Coach Parking: Yes
Length of Visit: 2 - 4 Hours
Booking Contact: Rosemary Mayhew
Bedgebury Pinetum, Park Lane, Goudhurst, Nr Cranbrook, Kent, TN17 2SL
Telephone: 01580 211781   Fax: 01580 212423
Email: rosemary.mayhew@forestry.gsi.gov.uk
Website: www.bedgeburypinetum.org.uk
Location: Signposted from the A21, north of Flimwell on the B2079

Please quote this guide when booking

There's magic and mystery, history and romance at this enchanting award-winning venue - which provides such an unusual combination of a traditional heritage garden with the contemporary landscaping of the ancient woodland.

First laid out in 1674 on a gentle, south-facing slope, the formal walled gardens are set against the romantic backdrop of a medieval moat house (not open to the public). They include herbaceous borders, an exquisite white rose garden with over 20 varieties of roses, a secret garden, knot garden, nut walk, paradise walk and oriental garden plus the drunken garden with its crazy topiary, and there's wonderful seasonal colour throughout spring, summer and autumn.

In complete contrast, in the ancient woodland of the 'Enchanted Forest' there are quirky and mysterious gardens developed by innovative designer, Ivan Hicks.

Fact File

Opening Times:	21st March - 5th November, daily 9.30am - 6pm (or dusk if earlier).
Admission Rates:	Adults £8.50, Senior Citizen £7.20, Child (3-12yrs) £7.00, Family Ticket (2+2) £29.50.
Group Rates:	Minimum group size: 20
	Adults £7.00, Senior Citizens July - August £6.00 (off peak £5.25), Students £6.00, School/Youth Groups £5.25.
Facilities:	Gift Shop, Licensed Restaurant, Plant Sales.
Disabled Access:	Yes. Toilet & limited parking for disabled on site. Wheelchairs on loan.
Tours/Events:	Guided tours for groups - pre booked only, £25 per guide. Major programme of Special Events throughout the season, including a Midsummer Garden Celebration 11th - 19th June.
Coach Parking:	Yes
Length of Visit:	3 - 4 hours
Booking Contact:	Carrie Hare
	Groombridge Place, Groombridge, Tunbridge Wells, Kent TN3 9QG
	Telephone 01892 861444 Fax: 01892 863996
Email:	office@groombridge.co.uk
Website:	www.groombridge.co.uk
Location:	4 miles south west of Tunbridge Wells on B2110, just off the A264 between Tunbridge Wells and East Grinstead.

Please quote this guide when booking

Hall Place is a fine Tudor mansion built almost 500 years ago in the reign of Henry VIII for the Lord Mayor of London, Sir John Champneys. It boasts a magnificent panelled Tudor Great Hall and Minstrels Gallery, and views over award winning gardens, with topiary, herb garden, secret garden, Italianate garden, Flora-for-Fauna garden and inspirational herbaceous borders. In its former walled gardens is a plant nursery and sub-tropical plant house where you can see ripening bananas in mid-winter.

A recent addition is the Educational Environmental Garden (wheelchair access), divided into Tudor Garden (looking at plants used for dyeing, medicine, beauty and cooking), meadow land, bug hunt ground and dipping pond.

There is a shop and numerous exhibitions, including an opportunity to purchase artists' work. Various rooms, including the Great Hall are available for hire for weddings and other events.

Fact File

Opening Times: Gardens: All Year, House: 1st April - 31st October Mon - Sat (10 - 5), Bank Hol & Sun (11 - 5), 1st November - 31st March Tues - Sat (10 - 4.15), Closed Sun & Mon.

Admission Rates: Free Admission

Group Rates: There is a charge for pre-booked guided tours.

Facilities: Gift Shop, Plant Sales, Teas, Restaurant.

Disabled Access: Partial. Toilet and parking for disabled on site.

Tours/Events: Pre-booked guided tours available of House and/or garden, A year long programme of events.

Coach Parking: Yes

Length of Visit: 3 - 4 hours

Booking Contact: Mrs J Hearn-Gillham
Bourne Road, Bexley, Kent, DA5 1PQ
Telephone: 01322 526574 Fax: 01322 522921

Email: jhearn-gillham@btconnect.com

Website: www.hallplaceandgardens.com

Location: Black Prince interchange of the A2, 5 miles from junction 2 on the M25, towards London, Nearest rail connection Bexley. Buses 229, 492, B15,132 to the foot of Gravel Hill.

Please quote this guide when booking

The Home of Charles Darwin, Down House   Kent

Down House was the home of Charles Darwin for the last 40 years of his life. It is here that he wrote about his theories on evolution and about more specific elements of our natural world.

English Heritage have been recreating the gardens as the Darwins would have seen them. Although small in size many elements of bigger gardens exist including bedding, shrubberies and mixed borders, an orchard, and a traditional kitchen garden and greenhouse. Victorian plant varieties are used throughout the garden, adding to the period feel.

The gardens are of special merit due to the scientific work Darwin undertook. He used the gardens and surrounding countryside to help prove his theories on evolution and looked for answers to his questions in the natural world. To demonstrate this, key experiments have been recreated to give the gardens the scientific feel they had in Darwin's time.

Fact File

Opening Times:	24th March - 30th Sept: 10am - 6pm Wed - Sun + Bank Holidays.
	1st Oct - 31st Oct 10am - 5pm Wed - Sun. Closed 1st Nov - 31st March.
Admission Rates:	Adults £6.60, Senior Citizen £5.00, Child £3.30. English Heritage members Free.
Groups Rates:	Minimum group size: 11 +
	15% discount for groups - drivers and leaders free.
Facilities:	Tearooms, Hospitality & Corporate Hire, Events, Shop, Audio Guide, Plant & Vegetable Sales.
Disabled Access:	Yes, Toilet and Parking for disabled on site.
Tours/Events:	Guided garden tours available. Please call for details.
Coach Parking:	Yes
Length of Visit:	2 - 3 hours
Booking Contact:	Site staff
	Down House, Downe, Kent, BR6 7JT
	Telephone: 01689 859119 Fax: 01689 862755
Email:	None
Website:	www.english-heritage.org.uk
Location:	Luxted Road, Downe; off A21 or A233

Please quote this guide when booking

Lullingstone Castle and World Garden   Kent

Set within 120 acres of beautiful Kent countryside, Lullingstone Castle is one of England's oldest family estates. The manor house and gate house - which overlook a stunning 15 acre lake - were built in 1497 and have been home to the same family ever since. During 2005, Tom Hart Dyke - 20th generation of Hart Dykes to live at Lullingstone - is creating within the Castle grounds a unique and beautiful 'World Garden' - which once complete - will contain 10,000 different plant species collected from all over the world. Tom designed the garden whilst being held hostage at gunpoint in the Colombian jungle for nine months in 2000. Five years later his designs are becoming reality and Tom would like to offer your group a unique and personal tour with him around the garden. Throughout 2005 the BBC are filming a television documentary series on Tom and the creation of his 'World Garden'.

Fact File

Opening Times: 1st April to 30th October. Fridays and Saturdays 12pm - 5pm, Sundays 2pm - 6pm. Pre-booked groups are also welcomed on Wednesdays and Thursdays.

Admission Rates: House & Grounds Adults £5.50, Senior Citizen £5.00, Child £2.50, Family £12.50.

Group Rates: Minimum group size: 15
Adults £4.50 per person plus £35.00 per group for Tom or a dedicated guide.

Facilities: Toilets, book and plant sales on site. Visitor Centre and cafe 400m easy stroll alongside River Darent.

Disabled Access: Yes. Toilet and parking for disabled on site.

Tours/Events: A Special group tour with Tom Hart Dyke may be booked in advance. Rare Plant Fair 12th June 2005

Coach Parking: Yes.

Length of Visit: Guided tour of House and Garden lasts approximately 2 hours.

Booking Contact: Mr and Mrs G Hart Dyke
Lullingstone Castle, Eynsford, Kent DA4 0JA.
Tel: 01322 862114 Fax: 01322 862115

Email: mail@publicity-works.org

Website: www.lullingstonecastle.co.uk

Location: Off the A225 near the village of Eynsford and just 10 minutes drive from Junction 3 of M25.

Please quote this guide when booking

Penshurst Place & Gardens Kent

Ancestral home of the Sidney family since 1552, with a history going back six and half centuries, Penshurst Place has been described as "the grandest and most perfectly preserved example of a fortified manor house in all England".

See the awe-inspiring Barons Hall with its 60ft high steeply angled roof and the State Rooms filled with fine tapestries, furniture, portraits and armour. The 11 acres of Gardens are as old as the original house - the walls and terraces were added in the Elizabethan era - and are divided into a series of self-contained garden rooms. Each garden room offers an abundance of variety in form, foliage and bloom and ensures a continuous display from Spring to Autumn.

There is also a Park with Woodland Trail, a Garden History Exhibition, a Toy Museum, Venture Playground, Shop, and Garden Tea Room, which contribute to a great day out.

Fact File

Opening Times:	Weekends from the 5th March, Daily from 19th March - 30th October.
Admission Rates:	**House & Gardens:** Adults £7.00, Senior Citizen £6.50, Child £5.00.
Groups Rates:	Minimum group size: 20
	Including garden tour: Adults £8.50, Senior Citizen £8.50, Child £4.50
Facilities:	Shop, Teas & Garden History Exhibition in Garden Tower.
Disabled Access:	Yes. Toilet and parking for disabled on site, Wheelchairs on loan, booking necessary.
Tours/Events:	Garden tours available for pre-booked groups.
Coach Parking:	Yes.
Length of Visit:	2 - 3 hours
Booking Contact:	Caroline Simpson
	Penshurst Place, Penhurst, Kent TN11 8DG
	Telephone: 01892 870307 Fax: 01892 870866
Email:	enquiries@penshurstplace.com
Website:	www.penshurstplace.com
Location:	M25 junction 5, follow A21 to Hastings. Exit at Hildenborough then follow brown tourists signs.

Please quote this guide when booking

Sissinghurst is a place that breathes old England, and yet the ideas behind its design, a series of intimate moments that together form a striking narrative - are very modern. Its Lime Walk, Herb Garden, Cottage Garden and above all the famous White Garden put on a kind of theatrical performance that marks the changing moods and colours of the seasons.

Vita Sackville-West and Harold Nicolson were an unusual couple - he a diplomat turned reviewer, she a writer and newspaper columnist who liked to work in a tower, not of ivory, but of warm pink brick.

Sissinghurst was originally built in the 1560's: once a poorhouse, and a prison, its Great Court was a ruin by the time the couple took it on in the 1930's. They built on the ancient template of a lost Elizabethan house to create a a bold new story: the result is a triumphant essay in English Style.

Fact File

Opening Times: 19th March to 30th October, Mondays, Tuesdays & Fridays 11am to 6.30pm. Saturdays, Sunday & Bank Holidays 10am to 6.30pm. Closed Wednesdays & Thursday.

Admission Rates: Adults £7.50, Family (2 adults 3 children) £18.50, Child £3.50, National Trust Members Free

Group Rates: Minimum group size: 11 - Please telephone for details. Booking necessary

Facilities: Shop, Self Service Restaurant, Exhibition, Picnic Areas, Woodland Walks.

Disabled Access: Yes. Toilet and Parking for disabled on site. Wheelchairs on loan.

Tours/Events: None.

Coach Parking: Yes.

Length of Visit: 2 1/2 hours

Booking Contact: Samantha Snaith
Sissinghurst Castle, Cranbrook, Kent, TN17 2AB
Telephone: 01580 710700 Fax: 01580 710702

Email: sissinghurst@nationaltrust.org.uk

Website: www.nationaltrust.org.uk/sissinghurst

Location: 2 miles north east of Cranbrook, 1 mile east of Sissinghurst village (A262)

Please quote this guide when booking

Squerryes Court Manor House & Gardens

Kent

The garden surrounding Squerryes Court is beautiful throughout the seasons. In 1700 the garden was laid out in the formal style. When the Warde family acquired Squerryes in 1731, they swept away most of the formal garden and re-landscaped it in the natural style then fashionable. The bones of the old garden survived.

Following the storm of 1987, the Warde family restored some of the formal garden using the 1719 print as a guideline. Hedges, pleached limes and a hornbeam avenue were planted. Box edged parterres containing lavender, santolina and purple sage were laid out. The Edwardian herbaceous borders were replanted. In other areas of the garden new borders have been created. The Victorian rockery features some fine topiary. The restoration is ongoing in the woodland garden, The lake, spring bulbs, rhododendrons and azaleas make this garden interesting all year. The manor house is also open.

Fact File

Opening Times: 1st April - 30th September, Wednesday, Thursday, Sunday & Bank Holiday Mondays. Garden open 12 noon, House open 1.30pm, last entry 5pm closes 5.30pm.

Admission Rates: House & Grounds, Adults £5.50, Senior Citizen £5.00, Child (under 16) £3.00, Family £13.00 Grounds only, Adults £3.60, Senior Citizen £3.30, Child (under 16) £2.00, Family £7.50

Group Rates: Pre-booked groups of 20+ welcome any day except Saturday, please telephone for details.

Facilities: Kiosk, Small Shop, Tea Room open 12.30pm for light lunches.

Disabled Access: Partial, please telephone for details. Toilet and parking for disabled on site.

Tours/Events: Please telephone for details.

Coach Parking: Yes.

Length of Visit: 2 hours

Booking Contact: Mrs Warde/Mrs White
Squerryes Court Manor House, Westerham, Kent, TN16 1SJ.
Telephone: 01959 562345 Fax: 01959 565949

Email: squerryes.court@squerryes.co.uk

Website: www.squerryes.co.uk

Location: 25 miles from London sign posted from A25. Half a mile west of centre of Westerham, 6 miles from exit 6 or 5 on the M25.

Please quote this guide when booking

Built as one of a line of coastal forts by Henry VIII as a protection against possible French invasion, since 1708 it has been the official residence of the Lords Warden of the Cinque Ports and the home of many famous men and women including the Duke of Wellington. Most recently, the Queen Mother made regular visits and stopovers here.

The gardens hold much of horticultural and historical interest. The moat that once surrounded the fort has been grassed over since the 19th century and now hosts a wide variety of flowers and other greenery. There is also a commemorative lawn, woodland walk, croquet lawn and a working kitchen garden, as well as a double herbaceous border flanked by mature yew hedges.

See the magnificent Queen Mother's Garden, designed by Penelope Hobhouse and given to Her Majesty on her 95th birthday.

Fact File

Opening Times: 24th March - 30th September 10am - 6pm daily (4pm Sats).
1st - 31st October Wed - Sun 10am - 4pm. Closed when Lord Warden in residence.

Admission Rates: Adults £5.95, Senior Citizen £4.50, Child £3.00. English Heritage members Free.

Groups Rates: 15% discount for groups - drivers and leaders free.

Facilities: Shop. Tearooms. Events. Available for private hire. Audio Tour.

Disabled Access: Partial: toilet and parking for disabled on site.

Tours/Events: Please call for details.

Coach Parking: Yes

Length of Visit: 2 1/2 hours

Booking Contact: Site staff
Walmer Castle, Kingsdown Road, Walmer, Deal, Kent, CT14 7LJ
Telephone: 01304 364288 Fax: 01304 364826

Email: None

Website: www.english-heritage.org.uk

Location: On the coast south of Walmer, Junction 13 off A20 or from M2 to Deal
Train : Walmer (1 mile).

Please quote this guide when booking

Yalding Organic Gardens   Kent

Described in the *Daily Telegraph* as 'among the most inspirational garden acres anywhere, for everyone', the gardens are rapidly gaining a reputation for being amongst the very best in the South East. Nestling against a traditional backdrop of hop gardens and oast houses, the gardens trace garden history through sixteen landscaped displays, including a 13th century apothecary's garden, a Tudor Knot, a cottager's garden in the early 19th century and a stunning herbaceous border, inspired by Gertrude Jekyll. Yalding is run by HDRA, Britain's leading organic gardening organisation, so naturally the gardens also demonstrate the best ways of making compost and how to control pests and diseases without using pesticides.

Kids will love the Children's garden. Home cooking is a speciality, using vegetables and salads fresh from the garden whenever possible - delicious! The gardens regularly appear on TV, most recently in Grassroots and the Flying Gardener.

Fact File

Opening Times: 10am - 5pm Wednesday to Sunday, May to September. Weekends only during April from Good Friday onwards and during October. Also open on Bank Holiday Mondays.

Admission Rates: Adults £3.50, Senior Citizens £3.00, Child Free.

Group Rates: Minimum group size: 14
Adults £2.75, Child Free.

Facilities: Visitor Centre, Shop, Plant sales, Teas, Restaurant.

Disabled Access: Yes. Toilet and parking for disabled on site.

Tours/Events: Monthly programme of pratical demonstrations at no extra cost.

Coach Parking: Yes

Length of Visit: 2 hours

Booking Contact: Events Office
Yalding Organic Gardens, Benover Road, Yalding, Nr Maidstone, Kent, ME18 6EX
Telephone: 02476 308211 Fax: 02476 639229

Email: enquiry@hdra.org.uk

Website: www.hdra.org.uk

Location: Half a mile south of Yalding on the B2162, 6 miles south west of Maidstone.

Please quote this guide when booking

Williamson Park

Situated in a commanding position over looking the city of Lancaster, Willamson Park has a variety of formal and informal walks through its 54 acre grounds.

The park was formally planted with many specimen trees to complement the striking rock formations, a legacy from the parks history as a stone quarry. Many of the trees which include *Linodendron tulipifera*, *Metasequoia glyptostrboides*, *Liquidambar styraciflua* and *Crinidendron hookerianum* where planted in the later part of the 19th century.

The parks centre piece, the Ashton Memorial, is a magnificent folly built by Lord Ashton in 1907. The building offers magnificent views over the surrounding coast and countryside, The park also has a Tropical Butterfly House and small zoo. All the facilities are open daily except Christmas, Boxing and New Year's Day. The park grounds are open throughout the year.

Fact File

Opening Times: All Year
Admission Rates: To Gardens Free. Adults £4.00, Senior Citizens £3.50, Child £2.50.
Groups Rates: Minimum group size 10
10% Discount
Facilities: Gift Shop, Teas, Cafe, Historic Folly.
Disabled Access: Partial. Toilets and parking for disabled on site.
Tours/Events: None
Coach Parking: Yes
Length of Visit: 2 Hours
Booking Contact: Elaine Charlton
Williamson Park, Lancaster, LA1 1UX
Telephone: 01524 33318 Fax: 01524 848338
Email: office@williamsonpark.com
Website: www.williamsonpark.com
Location: From junction 33 or 34 follow signs for Lancaster brown tourism signs from then on.

Please quote this guide when booking

A remarkable survival of English Garden history and the home of the Duke & Duchess of Rutland, Belvoir Castle and gardens are being sensitively restored to their former glory. The Spring Gardens contain a remarkable collection of Victorian daffodils planted sympathetically with primroses and bluebells, against a background of rhododendrons and azaleas.

Specimen trees of great rarity, many of them the largest of their type in the British Isles surround the newly restored rose garden.

Weekend events are held within the castle throughout the summer. Part of the great gardens collection.

Fact File

Opening Times:	March & October (Sundays only).
	1st April - 30th September.
	(Closed Mondays and Fridays, Open Bank Holidays).
Admission Rates:	Castle, Rose Garden & Duchess Garden - Adults £10.00, Senior Citizens £9.00, Child £5.00.
	Gardens only - Adults £5.00, Senior Citizen £5.00, Child Free.
Group Rates:	Minimum group size: 20
	Adults £7.50, Senior Citizen £6.50, Child £5.00, Family £26.00
Facilities:	Restaurant, Gift Shop.
Disabled Access:	Yes. Toilet and parking for disabled on site.
Tours/Events:	Weekend events - please telephone for details.
Coach Parking:	Yes
Length of Visit:	2 hours
Booking Contact:	Mary Mckinlay
	Belvoir Castle, Belvoir, Grantham, Leicestershire, NG32 1PE
	Telephone: 01476 871002 Fax: 01476 871018
Email:	info@belvoircastle.com
Website:	www.belvoircastle.com
Location:	Close to Grantham.

Please quote this guide when booking

Rockingham Castle   Leicestershire

Rockingham Castle stands on the edge of an escarpment giving dramatic views over five counties and the Welland Valley below.

The Castle architecture has examples from every period of its 950 year history. Surrounding the castle some 12 acres of gardens largely following the foot print of the medieval castle which houses the vast 400 year old "Elephant Hedge" that divides the formal 17th century terraced garden. The circular Yew hedge stands on the site of the moat and bailey that provides a backdrop for the Rose garden. Below the castle is the stunning 19th century "Wild Garden" that was replanted with advice from Kew Gardens. There are some 200 different species including a remarkabe AILANTHUS altissima "Tree of Heaven" some fine SEQUOIA and a good DAVIDIA "Handkerchief Tree".

There is something to see in the garden throughout the year.

Fact File

Opening Times: Open 12noon - 5pm. Grounds open at 12 noon. Castle opens at 1pm Easter (27th March) to April on Sundays & Bank Holiday Mondays, May to September on Sundays, Bank Holidays Mondays and Tuesdays.

Admission Rates: House & Gardens: Adults £7.50, Senior Citizen £6.50, Child (5 - 16) £4.50, Family(2+2) £19.50 Grounds (Gardens, Salvin's Tower, Gift Shop & Licensed Tea Room) Adult & Child £4.50 (Not available when special events are held in the grounds).

Group Rates: Minimum group size: 20 Adults £6.50, School Groups Child £3.25 (1 adult free with 15 children)

Facilities: Shop, Restaurant.

Disabled Access: Yes. Toilet and Parking for disabled on site.

Tours/Events: Tours of garden with Head Gardener, Richard Stribley for booked groups of 20 or more.

Coach Parking: Yes.

Length of Visit: 2 1/2 - 3 hours

Booking Contact: Nicola Moss
Rockingham Castle, Rockingham, Market Harborough, Leicestershire, LE16 8TH
Telephone: 01536 770240 Fax: 01536 771692

Email: estateoffice@rockinghamcastle.com

Website: www.rockinghamcastle.com

Location: 1 mile north of Corby A6003.

Please quote this guide when booking

A traditional country house garden, with inner gardens sheltered with yew hedges. They contain a Rose Garden with a good collection of old and new Roses, a White Garden, Herbaceous Borders and a Purple Border.

The central garden leads to spring and woodland gardens around a series of ponds, planted with trillium, arisaema, primulas and a multitude of spring bulbs and ferns, Beyond, a new arboretum and woodland walk.

The main Arboretum has an interesting collection of trees and shrubs and leads from the Clock House to the end of the front drive on the north side. A well designed Vegetable Garden and Orchard leads from the Main Garden through a Hornbeam tunnel with Hellebores, Hostas and Allium; Geometric border patterns for vegetables and arches of Roses and Clematis. The Orchard centre has a large Arbour planted with red Vines and red climbing Roses.

Fact File

Opening Times:	Sunday 27th February - "Promise of Spring" plant & bulb sales 11am - 3pm.
	Every Tuesdays 5th April - 26th July 9.30am - 12.30pm (RHS members free).
	NGS Openings: Sunday 24th April - Plant Sale 11am - 4pm,
	Sunday 19th June - Plant Fair (20 Nurserymen) 11am - 4pm.
	April to July every Tuesdays 9.30 - 12.30pm (RHS members free on Tuesdays only).
Admission Rates:	Adults £2.50, (£2.00 on Sun 27th Feb "Promise of Spring").
Facilities:	Refreshments - lunch, tea etc, Plant Sales.
Disabled Access:	Yes. Toilet and parking for disabled on site. Suitable for wheelchairs.
Tours/Events:	None.
Coach Parking:	Yes
Length of Visit:	1 - 2 1/2 hours
Booking Contact:	Wartnaby House, Wartnaby, Melton Mowbray, Leicestershire LE14 3HY
	Telephone: 01664 822549 Fax: 01664 822231
Email:	None
Website:	www.wartnabyplantlabels.co.uk
Location:	4 miles north west of Melton Mowbray. From A606 turn left through AB Kettleby 5 miles east of A46.

Please quote this guide when booking

12 acres of beautiful 'lost' gardens just off the A1. These important gardens have their roots in the mediaeval period, and the historical connections with both plant hunters and presidents.

The Cholmeley family have lived at Easton since the 1500s and over three years ago the present Lady Cholmeley undertook a lifelong project to revive the gardens and secure their future. Formal terraces have been cleared of undergrowth, old stone walls restored and new vistas opened up. Upon this beautiful old structure a new garden for the 21st century is emerging.

Every visitor is welcomed by friendly well-informed staff and a fine tearoom in the cut flower garden offers home-made teas and light lunches. Combine a trip to Easton with Vanburgh's beautiful Grimsthorpe Castle (see page 93). A tailor-made day for your group incorporates both gardens. Prices from £6.50-£25 per person. Call either garden for more details.

Fact File

Opening Times: 12th - 20th February 2005 (Snowdrops) 11 - 3pm; 27th - 28th March (Easter) 11am - 4pm, Wed, Sun & Bank Hol Mondays, 3rd April - 28th Sept 11am - 4 pm.
Admission Rates: Adults £3.50, Children Free.
Facilities: Plant & Seeds for sale, Teas, Gifts. Pre-booked lunches.
Disabled Access: Yes. Toilet & parking for disabled on site. Suitable for Wheelchairs, please ring.
Tours/Events: Pre-booked tours & workshops with owner/head gardener offered throughout the year. Snowdrops in February.
Coach Parking: Yes
Length of Visit: 1 - 2 1/2 hours
Booking Contact: Jude Hudson,
Easton Walled Gardens, Easton, Grantham, Lincs NG33 5AP.
Telephone 01476 530063 Fax: 01476 550116
Email: info@eastonwalledgardens.co.uk
Website: www.eastonwalledgardens.co.uk
Location: Just off the A1, north of Colsterworth roundabout turn right along B6403 follow signs to Easton, 1 mile on left.

Please quote this guide when booking

Discover the hidden delights of Grimsthorpe Castle Gardens. Immaculately clipped yew hedges and topiary squares sit comfortably alongside classic herbaceous borders. An unusual ornamental vegetable garden, designed in the 1960s complements rose parterres with clipped box edges. A mini-arboretum and wild, woodland garden await discovery. Cleverly positioned vistas extend across the lake to the 17th century tree-lined avenues beyond. This is a place to relax and enjoy the tranquillity of an historic English estate. The Castle is also open and contains a collection of paintings and furniture.

Combine a visit to Grimsthorpe with an opportunity to see the rejuvenation of Easton Walled Gardens (see page 92). We will produce a tailor-made day for your group incorporating both gardens, with a range of visit and catering options: Prices from £6.50 to £25.00 per person.

Fact File

Opening Times: Gardens & Park 27 March-30 May: Sunday, Thursday and Bank Holiday Mondays.
31 May - 31 Aug: Sunday - Thursday incl.
September: Sunday & Thursday 12noon - 6pm. (contact us for castle opening times).

Admission Rates: Adults £3.00, Senior Citizens £2.50, Child £2.00 (gardens only).

Groups Rates: Minimum group size: 20. For visits including a private tour of the castle, prices From £5.50 per Adult, (details on request).

Facilities: Tea Room, Shop, Information Room, Red Deer Herd, Woodland Adventure Playground.

Disabled Access: Yes. Toilet and parking for disabled on site. Wheelchairs on loan, booking necessary.

Tours/Events: Guided tour of 3000 acre park in your coach. Guided garden tours. Early evening private visits with candlelight supper.

Coach Parking: Yes

Length of Visit: 2 hours minimum

Booking Contact: Ray Biggs
Grimsthorpe Castle, The Estate Office, Grimsthorpe, Bourne, Lincs PE10 OLY
Telephone: 01778 591205   Fax: 01778 591259

Email: ray@grimsthorpe.co.uk

Website: www.grimsthorpe.co.uk

Location: Situated on A151, 10 minutes drive from the A1, nearest town Bourne (3 miles).

Please quote this guide when booking

Set in 300 acres of parkland and pleasure grounds, the Victorian walled garden is a unique experience. The garden has been carefully restored to its late Victorian heyday and grows fruit, flowers and vegetables dating from 1901 or earlier. Trained fruit, vegetable beds and cut flower borders are complemented by a range of glasshouses including a peach case, vinery, display house and fernery.

The huge herbaceous borders in the Secret Garden boast a colourful selection of unusual plants, whilst the Sunken Garden near the Hall is planted in pastel shades. There is also a parterre and rose beds, A 400ft long bog garden has been created in the base of the old ha-ha and a Victorian woodland garden is under development.

Fact File

Opening Times: Park open all year, 9am - dusk.
Walled Garden open 10.30 am - 5pm in summer, 10.30am - 4pm in winter.

Admission Rates: Adults £4.00, Senior Citizen £3.60, Child £2.00. (2004 prices)
Season Ticket admits 2 Adults & Children all year for £12.00. (2004 prices)

Groups Rates: Max group size: 30 Weekdays tours £32.00, Weekend & Evening tours £56.50.

Facilities: Visitor Centre, Shop, Tea Room, Restaurant, Plant Sales.
Regency Hall & Farm Museum also open 1pm - 4.30pm daily, during the season.

Disabled Access: Yes. Toilet and parking for disabled on site. Wheelchairs on loan, booking necessary.

Tours/Events: Guided tours of Walled Garden & Hall available - approx 1 1/2 hours
Special gardening events throughout the year.

Coach Parking: Yes

Length of Visit: 3 - 4 hours

Booking Contact: Mrs Sue Hoy
Normanby Hall Country Park, Normanby, Scunthorpe, North Lincs, DN15 9HU
Telephone : 01724 720588 Fax: 01724 721248

Email: sue.hoy@northlincs.gov.uk

Website: www. northlincs.gov.uk/normanby

Location: 4 miles north of Scunthorpe off the B1430

Please quote this guide when booking

Capel Manor Gardens   Middlesex

Capel Manor Gardens and estate provide a colourful and scented oasis surrounding a Georgian Manor House and Victorian Stables. It offers a unique opportunity to see behind the scenes at Greater London's only specialist College of Horticulture, Floristry, Garden Design, Equine, Animal Care and Countryside Studies.

The gardens are broadly divided into 5 zones, the largest of these is the historic landscape around the 18th century House and this includes a walled garden, wilderness area, magnolia border and 17th century gardens. There are extensive experimental and trials gardens within the complex, which are run by *Gardening Which?* Magazine. There is also a lakescape garden and an area of theme gardens which cover everything from topiary to flower arranging. All of this together with guided tours of the Exotic Animal Room make Capel Manor Gardens an excellent family outing. Capel also features two unique gardens: The Diana Princess of Wales Garden and Centenary Garden for HM Queen Elizabeth the Queen Mother supported by the Gardens Royal Benevolent Society now known as Perennial.

Fact File

Opening Times:	10am - 6pm (last entry 4.30pm). Open daily March - October. Please telephone to check times.
Admission Rates:	Adults £5.00, Senior Citizens £4.00, Child £2.00, Family Ticket £12.00.
Group Rates:	Minimum group size: 20 Adults £4.50, Senior Citizen £3.50, Child £1.50.
Facilities:	Visitor Centre, Shop, Plant Sales, Restaurant, Dogs allowed entry on lead.
Disabled Access:	Yes. Parking for disabled on site. Wheelchairs on loan, booking necessary.
Tours/Events:	Please telephone for details of tours and events programme.
Coach Parking:	Yes
Length of Visit:	2 - 3 hours
Booking Contact:	Julie Ryan Capel Manor Gardens, Bullsmoor Lane, Enfield, Middx, EN1 4RQ Telephone: 0208 366 4442 Fax: 01992 717544
Email:	julie.ryan@capel.ac.uk
Website:	www.capel.ac.uk
Location:	Near junction 25 of M25

Please quote this guide when booking

The Birmingham Botanical Gardens & Glasshouses   W Midlands

Opened in 1832, the Gardens are a 15 acre 'Oasis of Delight' with over 200 trees and the finest collection of plants in the Midlands. The Tropical House, full of rainforest vegetation, includes many economic plants and a 24ft lily pond. Palms, tree ferns and orchids are displayed in the Subtropical House. The Mediterranean House features citrus fruits and conservatory plants while the Arid House conveys a desert scene. There is colourful bedding on the Terrace plus Rhododendrons, Rose, Rock, Herb and Cottage Gardens, Trials Ground and Historic Gardens. The Gardens are notably home to the National Bonsai Collection.

Other attractions include a Children's Playground, Children's Discovery Garden, exotic birds in indoor and outdoor aviaries, an art gallery and Sculpture Trail. Bands play on summer Sunday afternoons and Bank Holidays.

Fact File

Opening Times:	Open daily from 9am (10am Sundays) until dusk (7pm latest)
Admission Rates:	Adults £5.90, Senior Citizen £3.50, Child £3.50
Groups Rates:	Minimum group size: 10
	Adults £4.80, Senior Citizen £3.10, Child £3.10
Facilities:	Shop, Tea Room, Plant Sales, Children's Discovery Garden, Sculpture Trail, Aviaries, Organic Garden.
Disabled Access:	Yes. Toilet and parking for disabled on site. Wheelchairs on loan, booking necessary.
Tours/Events:	Tours by appointment. Please telephone for details of Special Events programme.
Coach Parking:	Yes by appointment.
Length of Visit:	2 - 4 hours
Booking Contact:	Tony Cartwright
	The Birmingham Botanical Gardens, Westborne Road, Edgbaston, Birmingham, B15 3TR
	Telephone: 0121 454 1860 Fax: 0121 454 7835
Email:	admin@birminghambotanicalgardens.org
Website:	www.birminghambotanicalgardens.org
Location:	Access from M5 junction 3 and M6. Follow the signs for Edgbaston then brown tourist signs to Botanical Gardens.

Please quote this guide when booking

David Austin Roses   Wolverhampton

A large rose garden covering nearly two acres (0.8HA) and containing over 700 different varieties, considered by many to be one of the best rose gardens in the world. The garden is divided into five different areas each with their own style and mix of roses. (David Austin Roses are, of course, home to the English Roses and so are planted exclusively in the Renaissance Garden as well as scattered around the other areas of the garden). There is a particularly good collection of Old Roses and Climbers and Ramblers in the Long Garden and Wild Roses and thief hybrids in the Species Garden. Other plants that associate well with roses and are also found; clematis climbing up roses in the Long Garden and hardy perennials with roses in the mixed borders of the long garden; this garden also contains Hybrid Teas, Floribundas and English Roses planted in formal beds. There is something of interest twelve months of the year with flowers on the early Species in March through to the last flowers of the season on the repeat flowering roses braving the elements in November and December.

Fact File

Opening Times:	9am - 5pm (7 days a week) (Garden and Garden Shop)
	9.30am - 4.30pm Tea Room
Admission Rates:	Free entry
Groups Rates:	Free entry (Mon - Fri)
Facilities:	Shop, Plant Sales, Teas and Light Lunches
Disabled Access:	Yes. Parking for disabled on site.
Tours/Events:	Workshops with the RHS and Guided Tours (At a Small Charge)
Coach Parking:	Yes
Length of Visit:	2 - 3 Hours
Booking Contact:	Christobel Timmins
	David Austin Roses, Bowling Green Lane, Albrighton, Wolverhampton WV7 3HB.
	Telephone: 01902 376376 Fax: 01902 372142
Email:	plant-centre@davidaustinroses.co.uk
Website:	www.davidaustinroses.com
Location:	Albrighton is situated between the A41 and A464 about 8 miles west of Wolverhampton and 2 miles south east of junction 3 on the M54. Look for the brown tourist information signs.

Please quote this guide when booking

Ryton Organic Gardens   Warwickshire

The UK's premier centre for organic gardening, now with - The Vegetable Kingdom - a family friendly, fully interactive visitor centre telling the story of Britain's vegetables and the importance of preserving rare varieties.

Outside there are ten acres of gardens, including stunning flower borders, herbs, shrubs, a delightful children's garden and, of course, lots of interesting and unusual vegetables and fruit.

Also, learn the best ways of making compost and how to control pests, diseases and weeds without using chemicals.

Enjoy a delicious home cooked meal in our restaurant, or relax with organic cappuccino in the garden cafe. A greatly enlarged new shop provides lots to tempt you!

Fact File

Opening Times: 9am - 5pm.
Admission Rates: Adults £4.50, Senior Citizen £4.00, Child £2.00 (2004)
Facilities: Visitor Centre, Shop, Plant Sales, Teas, Restaurant.
Disabled Access: Yes. Toilet and Parking for disabled on site. Wheelchairs on loan, booking necessary.
Tours/Events: Regular programme of events, tours bookable.
Coach Parking: Yes.
Length of Visit: Half a day
Booking Contact: Events Office.
Ryton Organic Gardens, Coventry, CV8 3LG.
Telephone: 02476 308211 Fax: 02476 639229
Email: enquiry@hdra.org.uk
Website: www.hdra.org.uk
Location: Off The A45 on the road to Wolston 5 miles south east of Coventry.

Please quote this guide when booking

The Bressingham Gardens   Norfolk

"There's always something different happening at The Bressingham Gardens" - a visitor's comments overheard. Not surprising when you consider that apart from the two renowned 6 acre gardens, the unique father and son combination, Alan Bloom's Dell Garden and Adrian Bloom's Foggy Bottom, there are now four new areas under development, creating a wonderful tour for professional, amateur and leisure gardeners. A virtual tour with Adrian Bloom can be enjoyed at www. bressinghamgardens.com of the Summer Garden, which contains the National Collection of Miscanthus, the Dell Garden, 47 island beds in a beautiful setting containing nearly 5,000 varieties of perennials, the Fragrant Garden leading to Adrian's Wood which is being planted exclusively with North American native plants and cultivars - to the final destination of Foggy Bottom, where visitors can enjoy the quietness among the maturing trees, shrubs and conifers intermingled with perennials and ornamental grasses. A gardeners' paradise indeed! Blooms of Bressingham plant centre and Bressingham Steam Experience (included in ticket price) also on the same site.

Fact File

Opening Times: 1st April - end of October, The Dell: daily 10.30am-5.30pm (4.30pm in October). Foggy Bottom: daily 10.30am - 4.30pm.

Admission Rates: Adults £6.50, Senior Citizen £6.00, Child £4.00

Groups Rates: Please telephone for group rates.

Facilities: Visitors Centre, Shop, Tea Room, Restaurant, Kiosk, Plant Sales.

Disabled Access: Yes. Toilet and parking for disabled on site. Wheelchairs on loan, booking advised.

Tours/Events: Tours available for both gardens - please book (small extra charge). Please call for details of special events.

Coach Parking: Yes

Length of Visit: 2 - 3 hours. For plant lovers, all day.

Booking Contact: Sue Warwick
Visitor Centre, Bressingham, Diss, Norfolk, IP22 2AB
Telephone: 01379 686900 Fax: 01379 688085

Email: info@bressingham.co.uk

Website: www.bressinghamgardens.com

Location: Situated on A1066. two and half miles from Diss, twelve miles from Thetford.

Please quote this guide when booking

Fairhaven Woodland and Water Garden is a haven of peace and tranquillity in the heart of the Norfolk Broads.

180 acres environmentally managed for the thriving and varied wildlife. Delightful in Spring; primroses, daffodils, skunk cabbage (*Lysichitum Americanum*), bluebells, followed by a spectacular display of the largest naturalised collection of Candelabra primulas in England, and azaleas and rhododendrons. An oasis in Summer, with boat trips on our private broad, flowering shrubs and wild flowers which attract several species of butterflies. Glorious Autumn colours and quietly beautiful in Winter with wonderful reflections in the still water.

A full programme of special events is available including our Green/Environmental festival. Please ring for deails or visit our website.

Fact File

Opening Times: Open daily 10am - 5pm (dusk in winter) also open until 9pm on Wednesday and Thursday evenings from May to the end of August (Closed Christmas Day).

Admission Rates: Adult £4.00, Senior Citizen £3.50, Child £1.50
Annual Membership: Family £35.00, Single £15.00, Wildlife Sanctuary £1.50.

Groups Rates: Minimum group size: 15
Adults £3.75, Senior Citizen £3.25, Child £1.25

Facilities: Visitor Centre, Gift Shop, Tea Room, Plant Sales.

Disabled Access: Yes. Toilet and parking for disabled on site. Wheelchairs on loan. Booking necessay.

Tours/Events: Guided walks or introductory talk for pre-booked groups. Programme of Special Events available, including guided walks, music in the Garden, Green/Environmental Festival and Halloween event.

Coach Parking: Yes   **Length of Visit:** 2 - 3 hours or preferably all day.

Booking Contact: Mrs Beryl Debbage
Fairhaven Woodland & Water Garden, School Road, South Walsham, Norwich NR13 6DZ
Telephone/Fax: 01603 270449

Email: fairhavengardens@norfolkbroads.com

Website: www.norfolkbroads.com/fairhaven

Location: 9 miles east of Norwich, off B1140. Signposted on A47 at junction with B1140.

Please quote this guide when booking

Hoveton Hall Gardens   Norfolk

Set in the Norfolk Broads area, the gardens offer an exceptional range of plants, design features, landscape and inspiration throughout the season for garden and plant lovers. In early spring masses of narcissi, including many rare and unusual varieties collected during the 20th century, flower in drifts by the lakes and streams in the woodland areas. From late April to end of may the fragrance of the azaleas and rhododendrons is spectacular on the woodland walks; the lake and Water Garden area has beautiful displays of candelabra primulas and other moisture loving plants. During summer, hydrangeas from deep blue to pale pink and purple flank the sides of the main drive whilst the herbaceous borders and Clematis Walk are at their height of displays.

With, lakes, streams and wetland areas meandering through the estate together with a large wood, the gardens are also home to extensive birdlife, both migratory and native species.

Fact File

Opening Times:	March 27th to September 4th.
Admission Rates:	Adults £4.00, Senior Citizens £4.00, Child £1.50 (5-16yrs).
Group Rates:	Minimum group size: 15
	Paid in advance £3.50.
Facilities:	Plant Sales, Teas.
Disabled Access:	Partial
Tours/Events:	None
Coach Parking:	Yes
Length of Visit:	2 - 3 hours
Booking Contact:	Barbara Buxton
	Hoveton Hall Gardens, Norwich, Norfolk, NR12 8RJ
	Telephone: 01603 782798 Fax: 01603 784564
Email:	info@hovetonhallgardens.co.uk
Website:	www.hovetonhallgardens.co.uk
Location:	Follow brown and white signs off the A1151 just north of Wroxham.

Please quote this guide when booking

Pensthorpe Nature Reserve is set in 500 acres of unspoilt Wensum Valley with miles of nature trails winding through ancient fen meadows and woodlands. A series of beautiful lakes is home to over 70 species of breeding birds, and dozens of migratory visitors pass through, including rare species like the Osprey and the Squacco Heron. A feature of Pensthorpe is the spectacular Millennium Garden, designed by internationally acclaimed plantsman Piet Oudolf, winner of Gold and Best in Show at the Chelsea Flower Show. His revolutionary style of naturalistic planting fits perfectly into the landscape at Pensthorpe, so it is difficult to see where the garden begins and ends. Deep borders of grasses and perennials planted in bold drifts create dramatic waves of texture and colour, and familiar English Herbaceous border plants are cleverly combined with exotic plants. Piet's designs take the garden back closer to the haphazardness of nature. As he says "My biggest inspiration is nature - not to copy it, but to recreate the emotion".

Fact File

Opening Times: Jan - Mar 10am - 4pm; Apr - Dec 10am - 5pm.

Admission Rates: Adults £6.00, Senior Citizens £5.00, Child £3.00

Groups Rates: Minimum group size 15, Adults £4.50, Child £2.50

Facilities: Visitor Centre, Gift Shop, Plant Sales, Teas, Restaurant, Heated indoor viewing gallery, Gallery housing art and craft exhibitions.

Disabled Access: Yes (Gardens fully accessible). Toilet and parking for disabled on site. Wheelchairs on loan, booking advisable.

Tours/Events: Vehicle-safari with commentary.

Coach Parking: Yes

Length of Visit: 2 - 5 Hours

Booking Contact: Brigid Harrison
Pensthorpe Nature Reserve & Gardens, Fakenham, Norfolk, NR21 0LN.
Telephone: 01328 851465   Fax: 01328 855905

Email: info@pensthorpe.com

Website: www.pensthorpe.com

Location: One mile from Fakenham on the A1067 to Norwich.

Please quote this guide when booking

Sandringham   Norfolk

A visit to Sandringham's sixty-acre gardens is a delight at any time of year. Woodland walks, lakes and streams are planted to provide year-round colour and interest; sheets of spring flowering bulbs, avenues of rhododendrons and azaleas, beds of lavender and roses, dazzling autumn colour - there is always something to see. Other highlights include the formal North Garden, Queen Alexandra's summerhouse beside its own cascading stream, sixteen species of oak and many commemorative trees. Guided garden walks offered regularly.

Open Easter to mid-July and early August to end October, 10.30am to 5pm daily.

Fact File

Opening Times:	Easter - mid July and early August - end October
Admission Rates:	Adults £5.00, Senior Citizen £4.00, Child £3.00.
Groups Rates:	Minimum group size: 20
	10% discount when booked and paid for 30 days prior.
Facilities:	Visitor Centre, Gift Shop, Plant Sales, Teas, Restaurant, Sandringham Museum (inc in ticket) Sandringham House (Extra Charge).
Disabled Access:	Yes. Toilet and parking for disabled on site. Wheelchairs on loan.
Tours/Events:	Guided garden walks offered regularly.
Coach Parking:	Yes
Length of Visit:	2 hours. (for Garden only, longer for House and Museum).
Booking Contact:	Mrs N Colman
	Sandringham, Norfolk. PE35 6EN.
	Tel: 01553 612908 Fax: 01485 541571
Email:	visits@sandringhamestate.co.uk
Website:	www.sandringhamestate.co.uk
Location:	8 miles northeast of Kings Lynn on A149.

Please quote this guide when booking

Coton Manor   Northampton

Coton Manor lies in peaceful Northamptonshire countryside providing an ideal setting for the ten acre garden. Originally laid out in the 1920s by the grandparents of the current owner it comprises a number of smaller gardens, each one distinctive, providing variety and interest throughout the season.

The 17th century manor house acts as a central focus for the garden with the walls supporting unusual climbing roses, clematis and shrubs while the surrounding York stone terraces are populated by numerous pots and containers overflowing with pelargoniums, verbenas, heliotropes, salvias and agapanthus. The rest of the garden slopes down from the house and is landscaped on different levels lending a natural informality. Old yew and holly hedges complement the many luxuriant borders packed with unusual plants (most available in the specialist nursery) and displaying inspirational colour schemes throughout the season. Water is abundant at Coton with natural flowing streams, ponds and fountains everywhere. Beyond the confines of the garden there is a magnificent bluebell wood and established wildflower meadow.

The widely respected *Good Gardens Guide* says of Coton 'This is a beautifully maintained garden of exceptional charm with unexpected vistas at every turn....there is something for everyone here'.

Fact File

Opening Times: Easter to end of September. Tues to Sat and Bank Holiday weekends. (Also Sundays in April and May) 12 noon - 5.30pm.

Admission Rates: Adults £4.50, Senior Citizens £4.00, Child £2.00.

Group Rates: Adults £4.00

Facilities: Restaurant available for group bookings. Tearoom serving light lunches and teas, Extensive nursery with many unusual plants mostly grown from the garden, Shop.

Disabled Access: Yes (difficult in places) Toilet and parking for disabled on site.

Tours/Events: Tours by appointment (Wednesdays), Hellebore weekends (early March), Bluebell Wood (early May), Rose weeks (last fortnight of June).

Coach Parking: Yes.

Length of Visit: 2 - 2 1/2 hours

Booking Contact: Sarah Ball,
Coton Manor Garden, Nr Guilsborough, Northampton NN6 8RQ.
Telephone: 01604 740219 Fax: 01604 740838

Email: pasleytyler@cotonmanor.fsnet.co.uk

Website: www.cotonmanor.co.uk

Location: 9 miles NW of Northampton, between A5199 (formerly A50) and A428.

Please quote this guide when booking

Cottesbrooke Hall & Gardens   Northampton

Huge 300-year-old cedars set off magnificent double herbaceous borders, pools and lily-ponds, whilst on the south front are formal parterres framing the vista towards the famous 7th century church at Brixworth.

There is a stately Yew Statue Walk and many captivating views over the lake and Park. Here too are pergolas, rose borders and individually planted courtyards. In midsummer, visitors enjoy the splendid array of planters, a sight not to be missed.

The magical Wild Garden is a short walk across the Park and is planted along the course of a stream with its small cascades and arched bridges. Here are the wonderful colours of acers and rhododendrons, with bamboos and gunneras.

A number of distinguished landscape designers have been involved with gardens at Cottesbrooke including, Robert Weir Schultz, Sir Geoffrey Jellicoe and Dame Sylvia Crowe.

Fact File

Opening Times: May 2nd to the end of September. May & June: Wed & Thurs 2pm - 5.30pm, July, Aug & Sept: Thurs 2pm - 5.30pm, Plus Bank Hol Mondays (May-Sept) 2pm - 5.30pm

Admission Rates: House & Gardens: Adults £6.00, Child £3.00. (5 - 14yrs)
Gardens only: Adults £4.00, Child £2.00 (5 - 14yrs)

Group Rates: No concessions, minimum charge applies for private group bookings.

Facilities: Tearoom, Plants for sale.

Disabled Access: Yes (Gardens only), Toilet and parking for disabled on site.

Tours/Events: Guided tour of house (45 mins), Garden tours by prior arrangement,

Coach Parking: Yes.

Length of Visit: 1 1/2 hours (Garden) 45 mins (House).

Booking Contact: The Administrator
Cottesbrooke Hall, Northampton, NN6 8PF
Telephone: 01604 505808 Fax: 01604 505619

Email: hall@cottesbrooke.co.uk

Website: www.cottesbrookehall.co.uk

Location: Cottesbrooke is situated 10 miles north of Northampton off the A5199. Easily accessible from the A14 (junction 1 - A5199) and M1/M6.

Please quote this guide when booking

The Alnwick Garden - one of the great wonders of the contemporary gardening world. The centrepiece is the Grand Cascade, a magnificent tumbling mass of water, ending in an eruption of fountains sending 350 litres of water into the air every second. A computer system synchronises four sensational displays that offer not only a visual treat but also an interactive experience for children who can play in the water jets.

Beyond the Grand Cascade lies the Ornamental Garden, a symmetrical, structured garden with a strong European influence containing 16,500 plants. Nestled in a corner of The Garden is the Rose Garden, with pergola lined paths covered in climbing and shrub roses mixed with glorious honeysuckle and clematis - the scent is heavenly. Joining The Garden this year will be one of the largest wooden tree houses in the world with an amazing elevated cafe and three new gardens. There's the Serpent Garden, with a wonderful array of water features and topiary, the bamboo Labyrinth and the Poison Garden, full of mystery and intrigue.

Designed by the renowned Belgium father and son company, Wirtz international, The Garden is the vision of the Duchess of Northumberland.

Fact File

Opening Times: 10am until dusk, every day except Christmas Day.

Admission Rates: Adults £4.00, Senior Citizen £3.75, Child under 16 yrs free when accompanied by an adult. (Prices valid until 1st April 2005).

Groups Rates: Minimum group size: 14
Adults £3.50, Children under 16 free when accompanied by an adult.

Facilities: Garden Cafe and Tree House Cafe, Garden Shop and Tree House Shop.

Disabled Access: Yes. Toilet and parking for disabled on site.

Tours/Events: Please telephone 01665 511350 for details of tours and special events.

Coach Parking: Yes

Length of Visit: At least 1 hour

Booking Contact: The Alnwick Garden, Alnwick, Northumberland, NE66 1YU
Telephone: 01665 511350 Fax: 01665 511351

Email: info@alnwickgarden.com

Website: www.alnwickgarden.com

Location: Leave the A1 North of the town at the junction signposted by the tourist information sign for The Alnwick Garden. The Garden is clearly signposted, approximately 1 mile from the A1 junction.

Please quote this guide when booking

Cragside   Northumberland

Cragside has one of the finest high Victorian gardens in the country open to visitors. The rock garden is one of the largest in Europe and is probably the last surviving example of its type.

A fine collection of conifers, mainly from North America, is to be found in the Pinetum, below Cragside House, and across the valley lie the three terraces of the Formal Garden. On the top terrace is the Orchard House, the only remaining glass house in the gardens, which was built for the culture of early fruit. Nearby are the stone-framed carpet beds, planted for the summer season and on the middle terrace just below is the Dahlia Walk. Restoration is still in progress on the bottom, or Italian Terrace, which contains a wonderful loggia and an imposing quatre-foil pool. Finally, the Valley Garden itself is yet to be developed, but provides a wonderful setting for a gentle stroll.

Fact File

Opening Times: 22 March - 30 October, Tuesday - Sunday (and Bank Holiday Mondays).
Estate & Gardens: 10.30am - 7.00pm (Last admission 5.00pm).
House: 1.00pm - 5.30pm (last admission 4.30pm). Possible closure from 26 Sept for service renewal works.
Winter 2 Nov - 18 Dec 11.00am - 4.00pm (last admission 3pm) House closed.

Admission Rates: House, Estate & Gardens - Adults £8.50, Child £4.00 (5-17yrs), Family £20.00
Estate & Gardens - Adults £5.70, Child £2.60 (5-17yrs), Family £14.00
Winter - Adults £2.80, Child £1.30 (5-17yrs), Family £7.00

Group Rates: Minimum group size 15: must be pre-booked.
House, Estate & Gardens: Adults £7.00. Estate & Gardens: £4.70, Winter £2.30

Facilities: Visitor Centre, Shop, Restaurant.

Disabled Access: Limited. Please ring to discuss.

Tours/Events: Tours by private arrangement subject to availability. Please telephone for events programme.

Coach Parking: Yes **Length of Visit:** minimum 3 hours

Booking Contact: Val Miller. Cragside, Rothbury, Morpeth, Northumberland, NE65 7PX
Telephone: 01669 622001 Fax: 01669 620066

Email: val.miller@nationaltrust.org.uk **Website:** www.nationaltrust.org.uk

Location: Entrance 1 mile N of Rotherbury (B6341). 15 miles NW of Morpeth, 13 miles SW of Alnwick.

Please quote this guide when booking

In 2004 *Country Life* Magazine voted Buscot Park one of the best water gardens in England. The Water Garden was laid out by Harold Peto in 1904 for the 1st Lord Faringdon. Peto was the leading exponent of formal Italianate garden design of his day and intended the Water Garden to create a link between the eighteenth century house and the lake.

Designed as a descending canal between woods on either side, it is carved out within a grass walkway, lined with box hedges which widen at intervals to allow the canal to expand into formal rectangular pools. Statues, seats and fastigiate yews flank the hedges and the descent is punctuated by stone steps, footbridges and occasional fountains. Elsewhere in the park the present Lord Faringdon continues to enhance the landscape and has recently transformed the redundant kitchen gardens into a ravishing ornamental garden approached through spectacular year-round borders planted by Peter Coates in 1986.

Fact File

Opening Times: Please Call 0845 345 3387 for details. (25th Mar - 30th Sept)
Admission Rates: Adults £6.50 (House & Gardens) £4.50 (Gardens Only), Child 1/2 Adult price.
Group Rates: None
Facilities: Teas, Occasional plant sales. PYO soft fruit in season - tel 01367 245705.
Disabled Access: Partial, Toilet and parking for disabled on site. Wheelchairs on loan, booking necessary.
Tours/Events: None
Coach Parking: Yes.
Length of Visit: 3 hours
Booking Contact: Estate Office
Buscot Park, Faringdon, Oxfordshire, SN7 8BU.
Telephone: 01367 240786 Fax: 01367 241794
Email: estbuscot@aol.com
Website: www.buscot-park.com
Location: Buscot Park is on the A417 between Faringdon and Lechlade. It is marked on most larger scale road maps.

Please quote this guide when booking

Following extensive developments the Park has become an unexpected attraction to gardeners. Always a family favourite with animal lovers, garden lovers are surprised at the rich diversity of plants and planting styles encountered throughout the 160 acres of landscaped parkland surrounding a listed Victorian Manor House. The Victorian residents would have been familiar with formal parterres and traditional herbaceous borders but not the exuberant and stunning summer displays of hardy and tender exotics including huge bananas and flamboyant cannas now found in what was once the Walled Kitchen Garden. The unique arid-scape of cactus and succulents surrounding the meerkats, the calls of Kookaburras, Lemurs and Macaws give this area a truly tropical ambience. The flower meadows of snowdrops, narcissus and bluebells, so welcome in the spring, contrast with the large sweeping groups of ornamental grasses and perennials which provide a wonderful foil for rhino and zebras and the many different types of bamboo which feature strongly in other animal enclosures.

Fact File

Opening Times:	Everyday (except Christmas Day). 10am. (last admission 3pm October - February).
Admission Rates:	Adults £8.50, Senior Citizens £6.00, Child £6.00, (3-16yrs).
Group Rates:	Minimum group size: 20 Adults £7.00, Senior Citizen £5.00, Child £4.50.
Facilities:	Shop, Teas, Restaurant. (Restaurant available for booked lunches and teas, waitress service in Orangery).
Disabled Access:	Yes. Parking for disabled on site. Wheelchairs on loan, booking necessary.
Tours/Events:	Gardens Special for inclusive charge, talk by Head Gardener or his Deputy in the Drawing room of the Manor House and Cotswold Cream Teas in the Orangery.
Coach Parking:	Yes
Length of Visit:	2 1/2 - 3 hours
Booking Contact:	General Office. Cotswold Wildlife Park, Burford, Oxfordshire, OX18 4JW Telephone: 01993 823006 Fax: 01993 823807
Email:	None
Website:	www.cotswoldwildlifepark.co.uk
Location:	On A361 2.5 miles south of A40 at Burford.

Please quote this guide when booking

ROUSHAM and its landscape garden should be a place of pilgrimage for students of the work of William Kent (1685 - 1748).

Rousham represents the first phase of English landscape design and remains almost as Kent left it, one of the few gardens of this date to have escaped alteration, with many features which delighted eighteenth century visitors to Rousham still in situ.

The house, built in 1635 by Sir Robert Dormer, is still in the ownership of the same family. Kent added the wings and the stable block. Don't miss the walled garden with their herbacious borders, small parterre, pigeon house and espalier trees. A fine herd of rare Long-Horn cattle are to be seen in the park.

Rousham is uncommercial and unspoilt with no tea room and no shop. Bring a picnic, wear comfortable shoes and its yours for the day.

Fact File

Opening Times:	Every Day All Year
Admission Rates:	Adults £4.00, Senior Citizen £4.00, No Children under 15.
Groups Rates:	None
Facilities:	None
Disabled Access:	Partial, parking for disabled on site.
Tours/Events:	None
Coach Parking:	Yes
Length of Visit:	1 - 2 hours.
Booking Contact:	C Cottrell - Dormer
	Rousham, Nr Steeple Aston, Bicester, Oxon, OX25 4QX.
	Tel: 01869 347110 Fax: 01869 347110
Email:	None
Website:	www.rousham.org
Location:	South of B4030, East of A4260.

Please quote this guide when booking

Sulgrave Manor

Northants

Sulgrave Manor is a superb example of a modest manor house and garden of the time of Shakespeare, and was home to the ancestors of George Washington, the first President of the United States of America. In 1539 the manor was bought from Henry VIII by Lawrence Washington, and his descendants were to live there for the next 120 years. Sulgrave Manor was presented by British subscribers to the peoples of Great Britain and the United States of America in celebration of the Hundred Years Peace between the two nations. In 1924, the National Society of the Colonial Dames of America generously endowed the Manor House, and still co-operate with the board in its upkeep. Today visitors from all over the world, including many school children, come to enjoy this beautiful Tudor House set within the heart of a peaceful Northamptonshire village. The many attractions include the new Elizabethan Hangings. The individual designs have been embroidered by more than 500 volunteers from both Great Britain and the United States of America. Some motifs directly relevant to the sixteenth century.

Fact File

Opening Times:	April 1st - October 31st
Admission Rates:	Adults £5.75, Child £2.50,
Group Rates:	Minimum group size: 15
	Adults Variable
Facilities:	Gift Shop, Cafe
Disabled Access:	Partial. Toilet for disabled on site.
Tours/Events:	Yes, Please call for details
Coach Parking:	Yes
Length of Visit:	2 hours
Booking Contact:	Cheryl Moss
	Sulgrave Manor, Sulgrave, Banbury, OX17 2SD
	Telephone: 01295 760205 Fax: 01295 768056
Email:	sulgrave-manor@talk21.com
Website:	www.sulgravemanor.org.uk
Location:	Follow brown tourist signs from A43, M40 or M1

Please quote this guide when booking

Waterperry Gardens   Oxfordshire

Visit the fabulous Waterperry Gardens and discover ornamental trees, orchards, formal gardens, meadow pastures, hidden statues and the beautiful Mary Rose Garden, not forgetting our famous 200ft south facing herbaceous border.

Enjoy and purchase unique Arts & Crafts in our resident Art in Action Gallery then visit the Country Life Museum featuring interesting agricultural implements and aspects of local history. In the garden shop choose from a range of garden equipment, seeds and bulbs, country wear, locally grown fruits, books and an attractive range of gifts and mementos. New and experienced gardeners will marvel at the large choice of top quality, Waterperry cultivated plants available in our Plant Centre. Finally enjoy some well earned refreshments in the licensed Pear Tree Tea Rooms where you can choose from a delicious selection of lunches, home-made cakes, pastries and beverages many utilising fruits, herbs and produce from our own orchards and garden.

Fact File

Opening Times: April - October - 9am - 5.30pm, November - March 9am - 5pm.
Admission Rates: Adults £4.00, Senior Citizens £3.50, Child £2.50 under 10's Free. (Nov - Mar all £2.00)
Group Rates: Minimum group size: 20+ booked in advance.
Adults £3.25, Senior Citizens £3.25, Child £2.50 under 10's Free.
Facilities: Garden Shop, Plant Sales, Teas, Restaurant, Art in Action Gallery Museum.
Disabled Access: Yes. Toilet and parking for disabled on site. Wheelchairs on loan.
Tours/Events: Tours can be arranged
Snowdrop Weekend 19th-20th February, Aster Weekend 24th-25th September,
Apple Weekend 15th - 16th October.
Coach Parking: Yes
Length of Visit: Approx 3 - 4 hours
Booking Contact: Main Office, Waterperry Gardens, Nr Wheatley, Oxon, OX33 1JZ
Telephone: 01844 339254 Fax: 01844 339883
Email: office@waterperrygardens.fsnet.co.uk
Website: www.waterperrygardens.co,uk
Location: 7 miles east of Oxford - junction 8 M40 from London. Follow brown signs.
Junction 8a from Birmingham.

Please quote this guide when booking

The Barnsdale Garden familiar to millions of BBC2 viewers as the home of Geoff Hamilton and *Gardeners' World* comprises of 37 individual gardens and features that all blend together by the linking borders into one 8 acre garden.

There is not only a wealth of different plants to come and see, in many different conbinations, but also an enormous amount of practical ideas for any gardener. On average most people spend about 3 hours in the garden before venturing over to the nursery where we sell a wide range of choice and unusual garden plants, many initially propagated from the gardens. So allow plenty of time to take it all in and then relax in our small and friendly licensed coffee shop which serves a very appetising range of hot and cold food and drink.

We look forward to seeing you.

Fact File

Opening Times:	March- May, September & October 9am - 5pm. June - August 9am - 7pm, November - February 10am - 4pm. (Last entry 2 hours prior to closing). Closed 23rd - 25th December.
Admission Rates:	Adults £5.00, Senior Citizen £5.00, Child Free.
Groups Rate:	Minimum group size: 11 Adults £4.00, Senior Citizen £4.00, Child Free.
Facilities:	Shop, Tea Room, Plant Sales.
Disabled Access:	Yes. Toilet and parking for disabled on site. Wheelchairs on loan, booking advisable.
Tours/Events:	Yes throughout the year. Courses and Events booklet available.
Coach Parking:	Yes
Length of Visit:	3 hours
Booking Contact:	Barnsdale Gardens, The Avenue, Exton, Oakham, Rutland, LE15 8AH Telephone: 01572 813200 Fax: 01572 813346
Email:	office@barnsdalegardens.co.uk
Website:	www.barnsdalegardens.co.uk
Location:	A606 Oakham to Stamford and turn off at Barnsdale Lodge Hotel and we are then 1 mile on the left.

Please quote this guide when booking

The Dorothy Clive Garden   Staffordshire

Set amongst glorious views of the Staffordshire countryside this beautiful garden, created by local landowner, Colonel Harry Clive for his wife Dorothy, embraces a varity of landscape features. They include a superb woodland garden etched from a disused gravel quarry, an alpine scree, a fine collection of specimen trees, spectacular summer flower borders and many rare and unusual plants to intrigue and delight.

A host of spring bulbs, magnificent displays of Rhododendrons and Azaleas and stunning autumn colour are among the seasonal highlights.

A fine tearoom, overlooking the garden, provides a selection of home baking and light lunches.

Fact File

Opening Times:	Saturday 12th March - Monday 31st October.
Admission Rates:	Adults £4.00, Senior Citizen £3.40, Child (11-16) £1.00, up to 11 Free.
Group Rates:	Minimum group size: 20
	Daytime £3.40, Evening £4.00
Facilities:	Teas
Disabled Access:	Yes, Toilet and parking for disabled on site. Wheelchairs on loan, booking necessary.
Tours/Events:	None
Coach Parking:	Yes.
Length of Visit:	1 1/2 hours
Booking Contact:	Mrs Marianne Grime (Secretary)
	The Dorothy Clive Garden, Willoughbridge, Market Drayton, Shropshire, TF9 4EU
	Telephone: 01630 647237 Fax: 01630 647902
Email:	info@dorothyclivegarden.co.uk
Website:	www.dorothyclivegarden.co.uk
Location:	On the A51, two miles south from the village of Woore. From the M6 leave at Junction 15, take the A53, then the A51

Please quote this guide when booking

Cothay Manor and Gardens Somerset

Five miles West of Wellington, hidden in the high-banked lanes of Somerset, lies Cothay, built at the end of the Wars of the Roses in 1485. Virtually unchanged in 500 years, this sleeping beauty sits on the banks of the river Tone within its twelve acres of magical Gardens.

The Gardens, laid out in the 1920's, have been re-designed and replanted within the original structure. Many garden rooms, each a garden in itself, are set off a 200 yard yew walk. In addition there is a bog garden with azaleas and drifts of primuli, a cottage garden, a courtyard garden, river walk and fine trees. A truly romantic plantsman's paradise. **Two stars in the Good Garden Guide.**

Picture taken by; Christopher Simon Sykes

Fact File

Opening Times:	May to September incl. Wed, Thurs, Sun & Bank Holidays - 2pm to 6pm.
Admission Rates:	Gardens only - Adults £4.00, Senior Citizens £4.00, Child (under 12) £2.00.
Group Rates:	Minimum group size: 20+
	Please contact us for information pack. All groups by appointment only.
Facilities:	Plant Sales, Cream Teas, (Groups 20+ catering by arrangement).
Disabled Access:	Yes (Garden) Partial (House), Toilet and parking for disabled on site.
Tours/Events:	**Groups only:** Guided Garden Tour lasting one hour.
	Guided house tour 1 1/2hrs. **The Manor is open to groups throughout the year.**
Coach Parking:	Yes.
Length of Visit:	1 1/2 - 3 1/2 hours
Booking Contact:	The Administrator
	Cothay Manor, Greenham, Wellington, Somerset, TA21 0JR
	Telephone: 01823 672 283 Fax: 01823 672 345
Email:	cothaymanor@realemail.co.uk
Website:	None
Location:	From junction 26 M5, direction Wellington, take A38 direction Exeter, 31/2 miles turn right to Greenham. From junction 27 M5 take A38 direction Wellington, 31/2 miles take 2nd turning left to Greenham.

Please quote this guide when booking

One of the top ten gardens in England surrounds a magnificent 12th century home. Built of golden Hamstone it is a beautiful backdrop for a fascinating garden which has its beginnings in the early 1700's one of the first landscaped gardens. Throughout the seasons each area has its moment of glory. The acres of Crocus, the Azaleas and Rhododendrons, the spectacular Bog garden, the colourful rock garden, and the series of cascades and ponds with the Ionic Temple serenely overlooking the herbaceous borders.

The walled kitchen garden supplies the restaurant and house with fresh vegetables and salads, and the year finishes with the beautiful autumn colours in the arboretum.

Forde Abbey is a remarkable place, with its combination of grandeur and simplicity, the quality of timelessness and of total sympathy with the countryside around, making it a unique garden with something of interest to everyone.

Fact File

Opening Times:	Gardens open daily throughout the year from 10am (last admission 4.30pm). House open 22nd March to end of October, 12noon-4pm on Tue -Fri, Sundays & Bank Holiday Mondays.
Admission Rates:	Tel: 01460 221290
Groups Rates:	Minimum group size 20, Tel: 01460 220231.
Facilities:	Visitor Centre, Shop, Plant Sales, Teas, Restaurant and Pottery Exhibition.
Disabled Access:	Yes. (house not suitable for wheelchairs) Toilet and parking for disabled on site. Wheelchairs on loan, booking necessary.
Tours/Events:	None
Coach Parking:	Yes
Length of Visit:	3 hours
Booking Contact:	Mrs Carolyn Clay Forde Abbey, Chard, TA20 4LU Telephone: 01460 220231 Fax: 01460 220296
Email:	forde.abbey@virgin.net
Website:	www.fordeabbey.co.uk
Location:	Signposted from A30 Chard to Crewkerne & from A358 Chard to Axminster. 4 miles south east of Chard.

Please quote this guide when booking

Hestercombe Gardens   Somerset

Lose yourself in 40 acres of walks, streams and temples, vivid colours, formal terraces, woodland, lakes, cascades and views that take your breath away.

This is Hestercombe: a unique combination of three period gardens. The Georgian landscaped garden was created in the 1750's by Coplestone Warre Bampfylde, whose vision was complemented by the addition of a Victorian terrace and Shrubbery and the stunning Edwardian gardens designed by Sir Edwin Lutyens and Gertrude Jekyll. All once abandoned, now being faithfully restored to their former glory: each garden has its own quality of tranqility, wonder and inspiration.

Fact File

Opening Times:	Open every day 10am - 6pm (last admissions 5pm).
Admission Rates:	Adults £5.75, Senior Citizen £5.25, Child (5-15yrs) 2 Free with each paying adult.
Group Rates:	Minimum group size: 20 Adults
Facilities:	Visitor Centre with Courtyard Cafe, Shop, Plant Sales.
Disabled Access:	Partial. Toilet & parking for disabled on site. Wheelchairs on loan, booking not required.
Tours/Events:	A wide range of events including Open Air Plays, Seasonal Gift Fayre and Natural History Walks. Garden tours available for groups.
Coach Parking:	Yes
Length of Visit:	2 hours
Booking Contact:	Mrs Jackie Manning Hestercombe Gardens, Cheddon Fitzpaine, Taunton, Somerset, TA2 8LG Telephone 01823 413923 Fax: 01823 413747
Email:	info@hestercombegardens.com
Website:	www.hestercombegardens.com
Location:	4 miles from Taunton, signposted from all main roads with the Tourist Information Daisy symbol.

Please quote this guide when booking

The garden at Milton Lodge, on the southern slope of the Mendip Hills, was conceived about 1900 by Charles Tudway, the present owner's grandfather, who transformed the sloping ground south of the house into the existing terraces, specifically to capitalise on the glorious views of Wells Cathedral and the Vale of Avalon. Rescued from the ravages of war by Mr and Mrs David Tudway Quilter, who inherited the house in 1962, the garden has since been restored to its former glory, with mixed borders, climbers, roses and yew hedges, sheltered by trees to the north and the south facing walls.

Opposite the entrance lies the Combe, a seven acre nineteenth century woodland garden, providing a peaceful oasis in pleasant contrast to the terraced garden nearby. Both share advantages of fine old trees and lovely vistas of the Cathedral and the surrounding countryside.

Fact File

Opening Times: Tuesday, Wednesday, Sunday and Bank Holidays. 2 - 5pm
Admission Rates: Adults £3.00, Senior Citizen £3.00, Child under 14 Free.
Groups Rates: Minimum group size: 10
Adults £3.50, Senior Citizen £3.50, Child under 14 Free.
Facilities: Shop, Plant Sales, Teas on Sunday & Bank Holidays and by arrangement for groups.
Disabled Access: Not suitable for wheelchairs.
Tours/Events: Tours by prior arrangement only.
Coach Parking: Minibus and SMALL coaches only on site. Others ring for details.
Length of Visit: 1 1/2 hours
Booking Contact: Mr D Tudway Quilter
Milton Lodge Gardens, Old Bristol Road, Wells, Somerset, BA5 3AQ
Telephone : 01749 672168
Email: None
Website: None
Location: 1/2 mile north of Wells. From A39 Bristol - Wells turn north up old Bristol Road. Car park first gate on left.

Please quote this guide when booking

Prior Park Landscape Garden   Somerset

Beautiful and intimate 18th century landscaped garden, created by local entrepreneur and philanthropist Ralph Allen with advice from the poet Alexander Pope and 'Capability' Brown, the garden is set in a sweeping valley with magnificent views of the City of Bath. Some of the interesting features are a Palladian bridge, three lakes, and the recently restored summerhouse in the glade. An ideal picnic location.

The Wilderness is final stage of restoration, which will commence in 2005; this includes the Serpentine Lake and water cascades, Gothic Temple and Grass Cabinet. A 5-minute walk from the garden leads on to the Bath Skyline, a 6 mile circular walk around the city.

There is no car parking at the garden, public transport runs to and from the garden every 15 minutes. Call for a 'How to get There' leaflet or download a copy from the website.

Fact File

Opening Times: 1st Feb - 29th Nov 11am - 5.30pm every day except Tuesdays.
                         3rd Dec - 31st Jan 11am - Dusk Fri, Sat, Sunday. (Closed 24th, 25th Dec and Jan 1st)
Admission Rates: Adults £4.00, Child £2.00, Family Ticket (2 Adults, 2 Children) £10.00 (NT members free).
Facilities: Refreshments April - September.
Disabled Access: Partial. Toilet and parking for disabled on site, call to book disabled parking.
Tours/Events: Events programme, call for details.
Coach Parking: No
Length of Visit: 1 1/2 hours
Booking Contact: Visitor Services Manager
                         Prior Park Landscape Garden, Ralph Allen Drive, Bath, Somerset, BA2 5AH
                         Telephone: 01225 833422 Fax: 01225 833422
Email: priorpark@nationaltrust.org.uk
Website: www.nationaltrust.org.uk/priorpark
Location: The Garden is a 30 minute walk from Bath city centre.

Please quote this guide when booking

Kew Gardens, now a World Heritage Site, continues to offer a paradise throughout the seasons. Visitors can lose themselves in the magnificent conservatories and discover plants from the world's oceans, mountains and deserts. Its wide-open spaces, stunning vistas, listed buidlings and wildlife all contribute the Gardens unique atmosphere. There are also great places to eat and shop along with a museum and art gallery.

Why not tie in a visit with one of Kew's famous seasonal festivals? This year starts with the Orchid Festival (Feb-March) where over 100,000 orchids brighten up the dark winter months. During the Spring Festival (April-May) there are over 2 months of flowering splendour on display. Gardens of Glass is this years Summer Festival, where unique glass installations will be adorning every corner of Kew's beautiful landscape. The rich autumn colours and harvest treats are on display in October. While at Christmas (Dec) Kew will be shimmering with lights and seasonal activities. For further details and exact festival dates contact Kew on the details below.

Fact File

Opening Times:	Open daily at 9.30am. Closing times vary through the season.
Admission Rates:	Adult £8.50, Senior Citizen £6.00, Child Free (under 17's)
Groups Rates:	Minimum group size: 10 (must be pre-paid)
	Adults £7.65, Senior Citizen £5.40, Child Free
	Pre-paid - Adult £6.00, Senior Citizen £4.40, Child Free
	(All prices subject to change from Feb 05)
Facilities:	Visitor Centre, Shop, Plant Sales, Teas & Restaurant.
Disabled Access:	'On-site'. Toilets and parking for disabled. Wheelchairs on loan
Tours/Events:	Five seasonal Festivals per year.
	Walking tours at specific times. Daily guided tours (11am & 2pm).
Coach Parking:	Yes.
Length of Visit:	2 - 3 hours
Booking Contact:	Travel Trade Office, Kew Gardens, Richmond, Surrey, TW9 3AB
	Telephone: 020 8332 5648 Fax: 020 8332 5610
Email:	info@kew.org
Website:	www.kew.org
Location:	Silverlink and District Line to Kew Gardens. South West Trains to Kew Bridge Station. Buses 65 and 391. Parking on Kew Road(A307) and in Ferry Lane Car Park.

Please quote this guide when booking

Part of the magnificent grounds of Loseley Park, the original two and a half acre Walled Garden is largely based on a design by Gertrude Jekyll.

The Garden features five exquisite gardens, each with its own theme and character. The award-winning **Rose Garden** is planted with over one thousand old-fashioned rose bushes. The **Herb Garden** contains six separate sections devoted to culinary, medicinal, ornamental, dye plants, cosmetics and wildlife. The **Flower Garden** is designed to provide interest and colour throughout the season. The **White Garden** is serene, idyllic and tranquil with the central water feature flanked by borders of white, cream and silver plants. The **Vegetable** and **Cut Flower Garden** has an amazing variety of common and unusual plants and has stunned visitors with its displays. The **Moat**, with its associated **Moat Walk** runs almost the entire length of the Walled Garden and is abundant with wildlife and pond plants.

Fact File

Opening Times:	May - September, Tuesday - Sunday 11am - 5pm. May and August Bank Holidays.
Admission Rates:	Adults £3.00, Senior Citizen £2.50, Child £1.50
Groups Rates:	Minimum group size: 10 Adults £2.75, Senior Citizen £2.25, Child £1.25
Facilities:	Lunchtime Restaurant, Courtyard Teas, Shop, Plant Sales.
Disabled Access:	Yes. Toilet and parking for disabled on site. Wheelchairs on loan.
Tours/Events:	House tours and garden tours for groups by arrangement. Special evening tours with wine, music and canapes - contact for details.
Coach Parking:	Yes
Length of Visit:	2 hours
Booking Contact:	Elizabeth Blake Loseley Park, Estate Office, Guildford, Surrey, GU3 1HS Telephone: 01483 405112 Fax: 01483 302036 General Information: 01483 304440
Email:	enquiries@loseley-park.com
Website:	www.loseley-park.com
Location:	3 miles south of Guildford via A3 and B3000.

Please quote this guide when booking

With over 240 acres of garden there is plenty to see during your visit to RHS Garden Wisley. Its diversity and horticultural excellence providing visitors with ideas and inspiration all year round have made it one of the world's favourite gardens. Colour begins early in the year with witch hazels among the first to flower, followed by bulbs, blossom, new leaves and then the rhododendrons mean spring is always spectacular. Summer hits the garden in all areas with Mixed Borders, Roses and tropical plantings making a highlight. Autumn is no less colourful, with amazing yellows, oranges and reds on all kinds of plants, making way for the structure and design of the garden to become evident on the trees and shrubs in Seven Acres, Pinetum and Arboretum. Lastly other interesting areas include the Vegetable Garden, Fruit Garden and Orchard, Glasshouses, Trials Field and Rock Garden. A visit is made complete by the Restaurant, Cafe, Coffee Shop, Orchard Cafe, the Shop with superb range of gifts and horticultural books plus the Plant Centre with over 10,000 plants for sale.

Fact File

Opening Times: All year except Christmas Day. Mon-Fri 10am - 6pm, Sat & Sun 9am - 6pm (4.30pm Nov - Feb). Bank Holidays 9am opening.

Admission Rates: (2004 prices): Adults £7.00, Senior Citizen £7.00, Children £2.00 (6-16), under 6 free, RHS members and 1 guest free. Carer/Companion of disabled Free.

Groups Rates: Minimum group size 10+
Adults £5.50, Senior Citizen £5.50, Children £1.60 (6-16), under 6 free.

Facilities: Cafe, Restaurant, Orchard Cafe, Coffee Shop, Plant Centre, Shop.

Disabled Access: Yes. Toilet and parking for disabled on site. Wheelchairs on loan, electric buggies need pre-booking, suggested route around garden.

Tours/Events: Guided tours Mon-Sat, £1.50 per person, group rate 10+ £1.00. Many events throughout the year, including flower shows, Apple Festival and evening events.

Coach Parking: Yes, special coach park, coach driver refreshment voucher.

Length of Visit: 4 hours

Booking Contact: Sarah Martin, RHS Garden Wisley, Woking, Surrey, GU23 6QB
Tel: 01483 212307 Fax: 01483 211750

Email: sarahmartin@rhs.org.uk

Website: www.rhs.org.uk

Location: In Surrey, on the A3 near to J10 of the M25.

Please quote this guide when booking

Gardens & Grounds of Herstmonceux Castle East Sussex

Herstmonceux is renowned for its magnificent moated castle, set in beautiful parkland and superb Elizabethan Gardens. Built originally as a country home in the mid 15th century, Herstmonceux Castle embodies the history of medieval England and the romance of renaissance Europe. Set among carefully maintained Elizabethan Gardens and parkland, your experience begins with your first sight of the castle as it breaks into view.

In the grounds you will find the formal gardens including a walled garden dating from before 1570, a herb garden, the Shakespeare Garden, woodland sculptures, the Pyramid, the water lily filled moat and the Georgian style folly.

The Woodland walks will take you to the remains of three hundred year old sweet chestnut avenue, the rhododendron garden from the Lowther/Latham period, the waterfall (dependent on rainfall), and the 39 steps leading you through a woodland glade.

Fact File

Opening Times: 16th April - 23rd October, open daily. **Closed Sat 30th July.**
Admission Rates: Adults £4.50, Senior Citizen £3.50, Child £3.00 (5-15yrs).
Group Rates: Minimum group size: 15
                       Adults £3.50, Senior Citizen £3.00, Child/Students £2.00 (5-15yrs).
Facilities: Visitor Centre, Shop, Plant Sales, Tea Room, Nature Trail, Children's Woodland Play Area.
Disabled Access: Limited. Toilet and parking for disabled on site. 1 Wheelchair on loan, booking essential.
Tours/Events: Tours Sunday - Friday (Subject to availability) extra charge.
Coach Parking: Yes
Length of Visit: 2 - 4 hours
Booking Contact: Caroline Dennett
                       Herstmonceux Castle, Hailsham, East Sussex, BN27 1RN
                       Telephone: 01323 834457 Fax: 01323 834499
Email: c_dennett@isc-queensu.ac.uk
Website: www.herstmonceux-castle.com
Location: Located just outside the village of Herstmonceux on the A271, entrance is on Wartling Road.

Please quote this guide when booking

Merriments Gardens

East Sussex

A garden not be missed - **Merriments Garden** at **Hurst Green** offers everything for the "Garden Lover's" day out.

Set in 4 acres of gently sloping Weald farmland, this is a garden of richly and imaginatively planted deep curved borders, colour themed and planted in the great tradition of English gardening. These borders use a rich mix of trees, shrubs, perennials, grasses and many unusual annuals which ensure an arresting display of colour, freshness and vitality in the garden right through to its closing in autumn. Also in the garden are two large ponds, dry scree area, bog and wilder areas of garden planted only using plants suited for naturalising and colonising their environment. It delights all who visit.

The extensive Nursery offers a wide choice of unusual and interesting plants for sale many of which can be seen growing in the garden.

Fact File

Opening Times: 1st April to 30th September.
Admission Rates: Adults £4.00, Senior Citizens £4.00, Child £2.00.
Group Rates: Minimum group size: 12 (£3.50 per Adult)
Facilities: Gift Shop, Plant Sales, Teas, Restaurant.
Disabled Access: Yes. Toilet and parking for disabled on site. Wheelchairs on loan booking advisable.
Tours/Events: None
Coach Parking: Yes
Length of Visit: 2 - 3 hours
Booking Contact: Alana Sharp
Hawkhurst Road, Hurst Green, East Sussex, TN19 7RA.
Telephone: 01580 860666 Fax: 01580 860324
Email: info@merriments.co,uk
Website: www.merriments.co.uk
Location: 15 miles north of Hastings just off the A21 at Hurst Green.

Please quote this guide when booking

Boasting England's longest water-filled medieval moat encircling seven acres of beautiful grounds and gardens, discover nearly 800 years of history at Michelham Priory.

On this peaceful "island of history" explore the impressive 14th century gatehouse, working watermill and magnificent (reputedly haunted) Tudor Mansion that evolved from the former Augustinian Priory. In the grounds ingenious planting of the landscaped gardens offers the visitor an ever-changing display of beauty, whatever the season, while the physic cloister kitchen gardens add extra interest. Recently featured in *Country Life* and *The English Garden*, the gardens at Michelham leave a positive and lasting impression on all who visit them.

Fact File

Opening Times: 1st March - 30th Oct, Tuesday - Sunday from 10.30am
Also open daily in August and on Bank Holidays.
Closing times, March and October 4pm, April - July and September 5pm, August 5.30pm.

Admission Rates: Adults £5.40, Senior Citizen & Student £4.60, Child £2.80, Disabled/Carer £2.70, Family (2 + 2) £13.80

Groups Rates: Minimum group size: 15
Adults £4.35, Senior Citizen & Student £4.35, Child £2.50.
Free admission for coach drivers and tourist guides on production of a 'blue badge'

Facilities: Shop, Restaurant, Cafe, Plant Sales.

Disabled Access: Yes. Toilet and parking for disabled on site. Wheelchairs on loan, booking advised

Tours/Events: Guided tours organised for groups on request. Spring Garden Festival 9 - 10 April.

Coach Parking: Yes. Free refreshments for coach drivers.

Length of Visit: 3 - 4 hours

Booking Contact: Frances Preedy. Michelham Priory, Upper Dicker, Nr Hailsham, East Sussex, BN27 3QS
Telephone: 01323 844224   Fax: 01323 844030

Email: adminmich@sussexpast.co.uk   **Website:** www.sussexpast.co.uk

Location: 2 miles west of Hailsham & 8 miles north west of Eastbourne. Signposted from A22 & A27. (OS map 198 TQ558 093).

Please quote this guide when booking

Pashley Manor Gardens East Sussex

The de Passele family built a moated Manor in 1262 and held the estate untill 1453, when it was sold to the forebears of Anne Boleyn. It is possible that Anne, second wife of Henry VIII, stayed here during her childhood. In 1543 the estate was sold to Sir Thomas May, who built the Tudor house you see today, the fine Georgian Facade was added in 1720.

The Gardens offer a sumptuous blend of romantic landscaping, imaginative plantings and fine old trees, fountains, springs and large ponds. This is a quintessential English Garden of a very individual character, with exceptional views to the surrounding valleyed fields. Many eras of English history are reflected here, typifying the tradition of the English Country House and its Garden.

Pashley now holds a Tulip Festival in May, Spring and Summer Plant Fairs, Summer Rose time, open air Opera, The Sussex Guild Craft Show and an exhibition of Sculptures lasting throughout the season.

Fact File

Opening Times:	5th April - 29th September, Tuesday, Wednesday, Thursday & Saturday 11am - 5pm.
Admission Rates:	Adults £6.00, Senior Citizen £6.00, Child £5.50.
Groups Rates:	Minimum group size 20
	Adults £5.50, Senior Citizen £5.50.
Facilities:	Shop, Plant Sales, Teas, Licensed Cafe, Light Lunches.
Disabled Access:	Limited. Toilet and parking for disabled on site. Wheelchairs on loan, Booking necessary.
Tours/Events:	Tours of garden available. Please call for special event details.
Coach Parking:	Yes
Length of Visit:	2 1/2 hours
Booking Contact:	Claire Baker
	Pashley Manor Gardens, Ticehurst, East Sussex, TN5 7HE
	Tel: 01580 200888 Fax: 01580 200102
Email:	info@pashleymanorgardens.com
Website:	www.pashleymanorgardens.com
Location:	On the B2099 between the A21 and Ticehurst village (Tourist brown-signed).

Please quote this guide when booking

Borde Hill Garden, Park & Woodland   West Sussex

Glorious heritage Grade II* Garden offers beauty for all seasons. Spring is heralded by magnificent magnolias, rhododendrons and azaleas, blending into summer with fragrant roses and herbaceous plants. In the autumn visitors enjoy rich colour and in the winter architectural splendour with the Victorian glasshouses offering warmth and interest.

The Garden is a plantsman's paradise, with rare trees and shrubs introduced by the great plant collectors over 100 years ago, mainly from the Himalayas, Andes and Tasmania. This unique collection of trees also extends to many woodland areas and includes native hardwoods and specimen trees. Enjoy the distinctive formal 'garden rooms', including the sumptuous Rose Garden and the romantic Italian Garden. Find peace and tranquillity in the informal Azalea Ring and the Garden of Allah, and drama in the sub-tropical Round Dell. Set in 200 acres of parkland, the Garden affords panoramic views across the Ouse Valley and towards the South Downs. Lakeside walks to explore and picnic.

Fact File

Opening Times: Daily all year 10am - 6pm (or dusk if earlier).

Admission Rates: Mid March - Mid October **-** Adults £6.00, Senior Citizen £5.00, Child £3.50.
Mid October - End Dec - Adults £4.00, Senior Citizen £4.00, Child £2.50.

Group Rates: Minimum group size: 20 +
Mid March - Mid October **-** Adults £5.00, Senior Citizen £5.00, Child £3.00.
Mid October - End Dec - Adults £4.00, Senior Citizen £4.00, Child £2.50.

Facilities: Gift Shop, Tearooms, Jeremy's Restaurant (Good Food Guide 2004), Coarse Fishing, Adventure playground, Dogs on Leads Welcome.

Disabled Access: Yes, Toilet and parking for disabled on site. Wheelchairs on loan, booking advisable.

Tours/Events: Special events programme throughout the year. Tudor House open some dates in Jun & Oct.

Coach Parking: Yes.

Length of Visit: 2 - 4 hours

Booking Contact: The Administrator, Balcombe Road, Haywards Heath, West Sussex, RH16 1XP.
Telephone: 01444 450326 Fax: 01444 440427

Email: info@bordehill.co.uk

Website: www.bordehill.co.uk

Location: From London, Junction 10a on A23. From Brighton 20 mins by road, 1 1/2 miles north of Haywards Heath railway station.

Please quote this guide when booking

Denmans Garden

Denmans Garden is a beautiful four-acre garden owned by renowned garden designer and writer John Brookes and is one of the finest twentieth century gardens open to the public. Denmans Garden remains his private garden where he tries out new ideas. New for 2005 we have a formal herb garden that John has created in the old walled garden and the newly renovated and restored Victorian Conservatory.

It is a garden full of ideas to take home, in fact, and which can then be interpreted within smaller home spaces. There is something about Denmans that is quite unique. Its display is not only to do with flower colour, but foliage forms, textures and of course as we move towards the autumn months, with foliage colours as well. Our plant centre continues to develop and grow and is fast becoming known as the place to track down the elusive rare plant one has been searching for.

Fact File

Opening Times: Daily all year round 9am - 5pm.
Admission Rates: Adults £3.75, Senior Citizens £3.25, Child £1.95.
Group Rates: Minimum group size: 15
Adults £3.00, Senior Citizens £3.00.
Facilities: Plant Centre, Cafe, Gift Shop.
Disabled Access: Yes, Wheelchairs on loan, booking advisable.
Tours/Events: Study Mornings/Guided Tours.
Coach Parking: Yes.
Length of Visit: 2 - 3 hours
Booking Contact: Clare Scherer
Clock House, Denmans, Fontwell, Nr Arundel, West Sussex BN18 0SU.
Telephone: 01243 542 808 Fax: 01243 544 064
Email: denmans@denmans-garden.co.uk
Website: www.denmans-garden.co.uk
Location: Situated off A27 (westbound) between Chichester 6 miles and Arundel 5 miles adjacent to Fontwell Racecourse. The nearest railway station in Barnham 3 miles.

Please quote this guide when booking

Leonardslee Lakes & Gardens   West Sussex

In Spring, the sumptuous blooms of azaleas and rhododendrons (some 200 years old) overhang paths lined with bluebells in this romantic 240-acre valley with walks around seven lakes.

Watch the wallabies, wildfowl and deer. Enjoy the glorious rock Garden, admire the art of beautiful Bonsai, and marvel at the collection of Victorian Motorcars (1889 - 1900).

Visit the extended 'Behind the Doll's house' exhibition. This shows a country estate and local hamlet of 100 years ago - all in miniature 1/12th scale.

The Clock Tower Restaurant for morning coffee, lunches and teas. There is a Gift Shop and a wide selection of Plants for sale.

Fact File

Opening Times:	1st April - 31st October 9.30am - 6pm
Admission Rates:	May (Saturdays, Sundays & Bank Holiday Mondays) £8.00, May (Monday - Friday) £7.00, April & June to October £6.00, Children - Anytime (5-15yrs) £4.00
Groups Rates:	Minimum group size: 20
	May (Saturdays, Sundays & Bank Holiday Mondays) £7.00, May (Monday - Friday) £6.00, April & June to October £5.00, Children - Anytime (5-15yrs) £3.50
Facilities:	Shop, Restaurant, Plant Sales.
Disabled Access:	No
Tours/Events:	Early May Bonsai Weekend & demonstration, late June West Sussex Country Craft Fair, mid July Model Boat Regatta.
Coach Parking:	Yes (Free)
Length of Visit:	4 - 5 hours
Booking Contact:	Robin Loder. Leonardslee Gardens, Lower Beeding, Horsham, West Sussex, RH13 6PP Telephone: 01403 891212 Fax: 01403 891305
Email:	gardens@leonardslee.com
Website:	www.leonardslee.com
Location:	4 miles from Handcross at bottom of M23 via B2110, entrance is at junction of B2110 and A281, between Handcross and Cowfold.

Please quote this guide when booking

Parham House & Gardens West Sussex

Nestling at the base of the South Downs, Parham Park is a beautiful Elizabethan House. A herd of black fallow deer, established here for over 400 years, graze the surrounding medieval deer park. From the House visitors find themselves in the Pleasure Grounds where flowing lawns lead to the Lake with vistas into the surrounding parklands and the Downs beyond.

The walled garden, itself the subject of major articles in the Country's leading horticultural magazines, contains herbaceous and mixed borders, vibrant in colour and opulent in style. Designed to excite for a long season, peaking in summer and late autumn, the textures of the borders echo the precious tapestries in the House.

Parham is justly famous for the long tradition of informal flower arrangements that decorate the House throughout the season, all of which are supplied from the Gardens where there are huge borders and beds and an almost kaleidoscopic sea of colour.

Fact File

Opening Times: Easter Sunday - end of September. Wednesdays, Thursdays, Sundays and Bank Holiday Mondays (August additional Tuesdays and Fridays). Gardens open, 12pm, House open - 2pm - 5pm (last entry).

Admission Rates: House & Gardens, (Gardens) Adult £6.50 (£5.00) Senior Citizen £5.50 (£4.50).

Group Rates: Discounted rates for group advanced bookings.

Facilities: Restaurant selling light lunches from 12 noon and teas from 2.30pm, Gift Shop, Picnic Area, Plant Sales, Shop, Brick & Turf Maze, Wendy House.

Disabled Access: Yes. Toilet and parking for disabled on site.

Tours/Events: Parham Garden Weekend, Sat 9th - Sun 10th July, Autumn Flowers at Parham House Sat 10th - Sun 11th September. (Special admission rates for both events).

Coach Parking: Yes. No Charge.

Length of Visit: 2 - 3 hours

Booking Contact: Feona Clarke, Parham House & Gardens, Storrington, Pulborough, West Sussex, RH20 4HS. Telephone: 01903 742021 Fax: 01903 746557.

Email: bookings@parhaminsussex.co.uk

Website: www.parhaminsussex.co.uk

Location: Parham is located on the A283 midway between Storrington and Pulborough, Equidistant from the A24 or A29.

Please quote this guide when booking

St Mary's House & Gardens West Sussex

From the small gravel garden with clipped box and yew, the path leads over a pretty stone balustraded bridge to the topiary garden in front of the fifteenth-century timber-framed house. The yew tunnel beyond the gate leads to the ivy-clad Monk's Walk. The top lawn is enclosed by herbaceous beds, while the lower lawn has clipped yew hedges and roses, with a beautiful *Ginkgo Biloba*, and lower down a small pond.

The Victorian 'Secret' Garden boasts a 40-metre fruit wall with the original heated pineapple pits and stove house, the Jubilee rose Garden in memory of the late Queen Mother, herbaceous borders and yew hedges. The Terracotta garden has been planted with Box, giving structure to the planned herb garden. The circular orchard is being restored, and a woodland walk created, with underplanting of bluebells and primroses. The original Boulton and Paul potting shed houses a rural museum.

Fact File

Opening Times: May to End September.
Admission Rates: Adults £6.00, Senior Citizen £5.00, Child £2.50.
Group Rates: Groups (of 25 or more).
Adults £5.50, Child £2.50.
Facilities: Gift Shop, Teas, Car Park.
Disabled Access: Partial.
Tours/Events: None
Coach Parking: Yes.
Length of Visit: 2 hours.
Booking Contact: Jean Whitaker
St Mary's House, Bramber, West Sussex, BN44 3WE.
Tel: 01903 816205 Fax: 01903 816205
Email: info@stmarysbramber.co.uk
Website: www.stmarysbramber.co.uk
Location: 8 miles NE of Worthing off A283 in Bramber, 1 mile east of Steying.

Please quote this guide when booking

Visiting West Dean Gardens, winner of the Historic Houses Association/Christies's Garden of the Year 2002, you are immersed in a classic 19th Century designed landscape.

Its 21/2 acre highly acclaimed restored Victorian walled kitchen and fruit gardens, 13 original glasshouses dating from the 1890's, 35 acres of ornamental grounds, 240 acre landscaped park and the 49 acre St Roche's arboretum are all linked by a scenic 21/4 mile parkland walk. Features of the grounds include a 300ft long Edwardian pergola designed by Harold Peto hosting numerous climbers. Restoration of late Regency flint and rock work around the river, rebuilding of the 1820's summer house and replacement of a lost Laburnum arch combined with a contemporary planting scheme make this an exciting addition to the already expansive grounds.

The Visitor Centre houses a quality licensed restaurant and an imaginative garden shop.

Fact File

Opening Times: Open daily March - October. March, April & October 11am - 5pm.
May - September 10.30am - 5pm.

Admission Rates: Adults £5.50, Over 60's £5.00, Child £2.00.

Group Rates: Minimum group size: 20
Adults £5.00, Over 60's £5.00, Child £2.00.

Facilities: Visitor Centre, Shop, Plant Sales, Teas, Restaurant.

Disabled Access: Limited. Toilet and parking for disabled on site. Wheelchairs on loan, booking necessary.

Tours/Events: Tours by appointment only.
Annual events programme, please enquire for details.

Coach Parking: Yes.

Length of Visit: 2 - 4 hours.

Booking Contact: Celia Dickinson
West Dean Gardens, West Dean, Chichester, West Sussex, PO18 0QZ.
Tel: 01243 818221 Fax: 01243 811342

Email: gardens@westdean.org.uk

Website: www.westdean.org.uk

Location: On A286 6 miles north of Chichester.

Please quote this guide when booking

Created over the last decade the gardens are mature and varied. Visitors can enjoy the delights within the different areas: The Courtyard with Elizabethan Knot Garden, The Walled Garden, The Courtyard, The Bog Garden, Riverside and Lake Walks amongst others.

Opened in 1996 the Walled Garden is a splendid example of individual 'garden rooms' one of the most spectacular is the Rose Labyrinth, celebrated during the annual Rose Festival in June when it becomes rich with colour and perfume. There are beautiful 'hot' and 'cold' herbaceous borders containing plants, nurtured at Coughton Court, which are also on sale to visitors.

Thanks to the enthusiasm of the Throckmorton family, the gardens are now considered to be some of the finest in the country. In fact, the gardens have now become as big a draw as the house itself.

Fact File

Opening Times:	Check visitor information line on 01789 762435.
Admission Rates:	House & Gardens: Adults £8.60, Child (under 16) £4.30, under 5's Free.
	Gardens only: Adults £5.90, Child (under 16) £2.95
Group Rates:	Minimum group size: 15 (paying visitors)
	House & Gardens: £7.50, Gardens only: £5.15
Facilities:	Shop, Plant Sales, Teas, Restaurant, Gunpowder Plot Exhibition.
Disabled Access:	Yes (Gardens only), Toilet and parking for disabled on site.
Tours/Events:	There is a programme of events from March to Christmas
Parking:	All Cars £1.00. Coaches by prior arrangement.
Length of Visit:	3 hours
Booking Contact:	Coughton Court, Alcester, Warwickshire, B49 5JA.
	Telephone: 01789 400777 Fax: 01789 765544
Email:	sales@throckmortons.co.uk
Website:	www.coughtoncourt.co.uk
Location:	Take the A435 from Alcester towards Birmingham, the House is signposted from the road.

Please quote this guide when booking

Ragley Hall the family home of the Marquess and Marchioness of Hertford was designed by Robert Hooke in 1680 and is one of the earliest and loveliest of England's great Palladian Houses. The perfect symmetry of the architecture of Ragley remains unchanged save for the spectacular portico by Wyatt added in 1780. The majestic Great Hall, soaring two storeys high, is adorned with some of England's finest Baroque plasterwork by James Gibbs dated 1750. Ragley houses a superb collection of 18th century and earlier paintings, china and furniture and wonderful ceilings decorated with Grisaille panels and insets by Angelica Kauffman. Do not miss the breathtaking mural 'The Temptation' by Graham Rust in the south staircase hall that was painted between 1969 and 1983. The Hall is set in 400 acres of picturesque parkland landscaped by Lancelot 'Capability' Brown and 27 acres of fascinating gardens including the enchanting rose garden, richly planted borders and mature woodland. Gardening groups are welcomed throughout the year and we offer tailor-made packages for visits, lectures and catering. Please enquire.

Fact File

Opening Times: 19th March - 25th September, Thurs - Sun + Bank Holiday Mondays. Open daily during School Holidays. Saturday and Sunday in October.

Admission Rates: Adults £6.00, Senior Citizen £5.50, Child £4.50
House included - Adults £7.50, Senior Citizen £6.50, Child £4.50. (Thursday to Sunday)

Group Rates: 20
Adults £5.00, Senior Citizen £5.00, Child £3.00
House included - Adults £6.00, Senior Citizen £6.00, Child £3.00.

Facilities: Gift Shop, Plant Sales, Teas, Hooke's Coffee House & Restaurant, Adventure Playground, Lakeside Picnic & Play Area, Jerwood Sculpture Park, Woodland Walks.

Disabled Access: Yes. Toilet and parking for disabled on site. Wheelchairs on loan. Booking advisable.

Tours/Events: Various events please call for details and visit www.ragleyhall.com.

Coach Parking: Yes

Length of Visit: 2 + hours

Booking Contact: Michelle Malin, Ragley Hall, Alcester, Warwickshire, B49 5NJ
Telephone: 01789 762090 ext 125   Fax: 01789 764791

Email: Info@ragleyhall.com

Website: www. ragleyhall.com

Location: Ragley lies 8 miles West of Stratford-Upon-Avon, 2 miles From Alcester off the A46/A435.

Please quote this guide when booking

Shakespeare Gardens Warwickshire

The Shakespeare Gardens contain many of the plants and herbs mentioned in Shakespeare's writing and are immaculately maintained by a dedicated team of gardeners. Each garden has its own unique character and reflects traditional gardening styles and practices from 16th Century to the present day. Features include the Cottage Garden, Orchard, Sculpture Garden, Maze, History of Gardening exhibition and Romantic Willow Cabin at Anne Hathaway's Cottage, Elizabethan style Knot Garden and historic Great Garden at Nash's House & New Place and Herbal Bed and Ancient Mulberry Tree at Hall's Croft.

The gardens have been enjoyed by visitors to the Shakespeare Houses for over a century. Now, for the first time, the Shakespeare Birthplace Trust is offering an escorted 'gardens only' tour of the grounds of Anne Hathaway's Cottage, Nash's House & New Place and Hall's Croft. The tour will last approximately three hours and will be led by an expert guide. Participants will also have the opportunity to talk to the Shakespeare gardeners on site.

Fact File

Opening Times:	Easter to September 2005.
Admission Rates:	Adults £9.00, Senior Citizen £7.50, Child £4.50.
	NB, Rates are for a tour of all three gardens and do not include admission in to the Shakespeare Houses.
Group Rates:	Minimum group size: 10
Facilities:	Gift Shop, Tea Room.
Disabled Access:	Partial. Toilet and parking for disabled on site. Wheelchairs on loan at Anne Hathaway's Cottage only. Booking Advisable.
Tours/Events:	Guided garden tours available.
Coach Parking:	Yes. Anne Hathaway's Cottage.
Length of Visit:	2 - 3 hours.
Booking Contact:	Sarah Harris/Trace Colledge (Group Visits Office)
	Shakespeare Birthplace Trust, Henley Street, Stratford-Upon-Avon, CU37 6QW
	Tel: 01789 201806/201836 Fax: 01789 263138
Email:	groups@shakespeare.org.uk
Website:	www.shakespeare.org.uk
Location:	Tours start at Anne Hathaway's Cottage, Shottery (1 mile from Stratford-Upon-Avon).

Please quote this guide when booking

'The WOW! factor is here in abundance' Alan Titchmarsh. 5 acre gardens of fantastic colour throughout the season. Lovely camellias set off a fabulous display of over 50,000 bulbs including an amazing display of tulips. A superb collection of irises follows in May with wisteria, laburnum and a growing collection of rhododendrons and azeleas.

Throughout summer, 2,000 different roses in bloom are a breathtaking sight continuing until the frosts, supported by lilies and alstoemeria. The beautiful double herbaceous borders have been compared to Monet's and the wooded river walk created contrast in scale, atmosphere and planting. A unique herb garden, a folliage garden, hydrangeas, many specimen trees and shrubs take you through to autumn colour and all against the dramatic back drop of Malmesbury Abbey. The ancient hill top town itself with shops, cafes and museum, adds even more for a wonderful day out.

Fact File

Opening Times:	11am - 5.30pm 21st March - 21st October.
Admission Rates:	Adults £5.50, Senior Citizen £4.75, Child £2.00
Groups Rates:	Minimum group size 20
	Adults £4.50, Senior Citizen £4.50, Child £2.00
Facilities:	Plant Sales, Teas.
Disabled Access:	Yes.
Tours/Events:	Pre-booked guided tours with owner available. Exhibitions and plays.
Coach Parking:	Yes
Length of Visit:	2 hours minimum
Booking Contact:	Geraldine Pike
	Abbey House Gardens, Market Cross, Malmesbury, Wiltshire, SN16 9AS
	Telephone: 01666 827650 Fax: 01666 822782
Email:	info@abbeyhousegardens.co.uk
Website:	www.abbeyhousegardens.co.uk
Location:	In Malmesbury town centre. Off A429 between M4 junction 17 (5 miles) and Cirencester (12 miles). Coaches drop passengers in centre of town, 3 minute level walk from garden. Cars follow signs for long-stay car park (free) from Malmesbury town centre. Garden is 5 min walk across the bridge, up the Abbey steps and entered left of Cloister Garden.

Please quote this guide when booking

Bowood House & Gardens/Rhododendron Walks   Wiltshire

The Bowood Rhododendron Gardens cover some sixty acres surrounding Robert Adam's magnificent Mausoleum. The first Rhododendrons were introduced by the 3rd Marquis of Lansdowne in 1850. His grandson, on retiring as Viceroy in 1894, created the main structure of the woodland walks, planting mainly hardy hybrids, many of which are unavailable today. Over the past forty years, the present Lord Lansdowne, and his father before him, have added many hundreds of new varieties. A collection of broad-leafed plants come from the island of Ghia; another group of plants were grown from seeds collected by Roy Lancaster at 11,000 feet in the Western Yunan in 1979. It also includes a further group of species collected in Sichuan in 1991, which were propagated by Jim Russell at Castle Howard. Planting and thinning continues season after season. This garden is where man and nature are in harmony. An hour or more strolling along the network of paths looking over a sea of bluebells, with magnolias and giant Loderii reaching for the light between the overhanging oak canopy, is where paradise can be found.

Fact File

Opening Times: House & Gardens: 19th March - 1st November.
Rhododendron Walks: 6 week flowering season, late April to early June.

Admission Rates: Adults £6.60, Senior Citizen £5.50, Child £4.30 (5-15yrs), Child £3.40 (2-4yrs).
Just Rhododendrons £3.70 Season Tickets Available.

Groups Rates: Minimum group size 20 (N/A for just Rhododendron Walks)
Adults £5.60, Senior Citizen £4.80, Child £3.70 (5-15yrs), Child £3.20 (2-4yrs).

Facilities: At House & Garden: Visitor Centre, Shop, Teas, Restaurant, Aventure Playgroup, Coffee Shop.

Disabled Access: Partial. Toilet and parking for disabled on site. Wheelchairs on loan, booking necessary.

Tours/Events: Pre-booked guided tours available. For 2005 Special Events please visit the web site.

Coach Parking: Yes

Length of Visit: 3 + hours (House & Gardens), 2+ hours (Rhododendron Walks).

Booking Contact: Mrs Jane Meadows.
Bowood House, The Estate Office, Derry Hill, Calne, Wilts, SN11 0LZ.
Tel: 01249 812102 Fax: 01249 821757

Email: houseandgardens@bowood.org

Website: www.bowood.org

Location: House & Gardens: Off A4 midway between Chippenham and Calne.
Rhododendron Walks: Off A342 between Chippenham and Devizes.

Please quote this guide when booking

137

Broadleas is a 10 acre garden on green sand soil which allows acid loving plants to thrive. Mature and semi-mature magnolias grow on each side of a steep dell. As good as any Cornish garden, it is stuffed with fine things normally considered too tender for these parts. There are large specimens of everything (much of it now 50 years old) - Paulownia Fargessii, Porrotia Persica, all manner of magnolias, azaleas, hydrangeas, hostas, lilies and trilliums of rare and notable species. It is a garden of tireless perfectionism, at its most stunning in spring when sheets of bulbs stretch out beneath the flowering trees. There is also a Perennial Garden, Sunken Rose Garden and Grey Border with a great variety of shrubs and exotic climbers and a Woodland Walk where a few tender rarities are hidden away for protection from the elements.

Fact File

Opening Times: April - October 2 - 6pm , Sunday, Wednesday, Thursday.
Admission Rates: April - May - Adults £5.00, Child £1.50, June - October - Adults £4.00, Child £1.50.
Groups Rates: Minimum group size 10
April - May - Adults £4.50, Child £1.50, June - October - Adults £3.50, Child £1.50
Facilities: Tearoom, Plant Sales
Disabled Access: No
Tours/Events: None
Coach Parking: Yes
Length of Visit: 1 1/2 Hours
Booking Contact: Lady Anne Cowdray
Broadleas Gardens, Broadleas, Devizes, Wilts, SN10 5JQ
Telephone: 01380 722035
Email: None
Website: None
Location: 1 1/2 miles from centre of Devizes on A360 Salisbury Road.

Please quote this guide when booking

Heale House Garden & Plant Centre · Wiltshire

Heale House and its eight acres of beautiful garden, lie beside the river Avon, at Middle Woodford, just north of Salisbury. Much of the house is unchanged since King Charles II hid here in 1651.

In January great drifts of snowdrops and aconites bring early colour and this promise of spring is followed by magnificent magnolias and acers that surround the authentic Japanese Tea House and red Niko Bridge. The garden provides wonderfully varied collection of plants, shrubs, musk and other roses, a working kitchen garden, all growing in the formal setting of clipped hedges and mellow stonework and particularly lovely in June and July. As summer turns to Autumn, Cyclamen, Nerines and Viburnums are in flower and trees and shrubs in the Japanese Garden display their brilliant autumnal foliage before leaf fall and the start of winter flowering shrubs and Hellebores.

Fact File

Opening Times: Garden: Tuesday - Sunday 10am - 5pm (open Bank Holiday Mondays) all year.
Plant Centre: Monday - Sunday 10am - 5pm all year.

Admission Rates: Adults £3.75, Senior Citizen £3.75, Child £1.50 (5-15yrs)

Groups Rates: Minimum group size: 20
Adults £3.50, Senior Citizen £3.50, Child £1.50 (5-15yrs)

Facilities: Shop, Plant Sales, Light lunches and cream teas available Thurs-Sun April - Sept.

Disabled Access: Yes.

Tours/Events: Snowdrop weekends, 6th and 13th February. Guided tour and hot food on these first Sundays in February of the Snowdrop and Winter Aconite display.

Coach Parking: Yes

Length of Visit: 1 1/2 - 2 hours

Booking Contact: Miss Fiona Walmsley
Heale House, Middle Woodford, Nr Salisbury, Wiltshire, SP4 6NT
Telephone: 01722 782504   Fax: 01722 782504

Email: None

Website: None

Location: Four miles from Salisbury, Wilton and Stonehenge, on the 'Woodford Valley' road between the A360 and A345.

Please quote this guide when booking

The splendour of Longleat House nestling alongside a lake and within rolling 'Capability' Brown landscaped grounds is a view that cannot be missed. Fringed by thousands of trees the grounds include formal gardens, a 'Secret Garden' the 'Pleasure Walk', a 19th century planting of rhododendrons and azaleas, topiary and fine examples of mazes including the Love Labyrinth, the Sun Maze and the Lunar Labyrinth.

A recent addition to Longleat are standing stones at Heaven's Gate - the massive stones and a ring-shaped 'gateway' - made up of 13 smaller stones - form part of a gigantic sculpture which was commissioned by the Seventh Marquess of Bath.

Fact File

Opening Times: Open Daily, (except Christmas Day) Easter to September 10am - 5.30pm, Rest of year Guided tours at set times between 11am and 3pm, may be subject to change.

Admission Rates: Please Telephone for details.

Groups Rates: Minimum group size: 12
Please telephone for details.

Facilities: Shops, Restaurant and Cafe.

Disabled Access: Yes. Toilet and parking for disabled on site. Wheelchairs on loan, booking necessary.

Tours/Events: See website for our specialist garden tours or telephone for details.

Coach Parking: Yes

Length of Visit: A Full Day

Booking Contact: Scott Sims
Longleat, Warminster, Wiltshire, BA12 7NW
Telephone : 01985 844328 Fax: 01985 844763

Email: enquiries@longleat.co.uk

Website: www.longleat.co.uk

Location: Longleat is situated just off the A36 between Bath and Salisbury (A362 Warminster - Frome).

Please quote this guide when booking

Romantically sited overlooking the valley of the River Frome, close to Badford-on-Avon, Iford Manor is built into the hillside below a hanging beechwood and fine garden terraces. The house was owned during the first part of the last century by Harold Peto, the architect and landscape designer who taught Lutyens, and who expressed his passion for classical Italian architecture and landscaping in an English setting. After many visits to Italy he acquired statues and architectural marbles. He planted phillyrea and cypress trees and other Mediterranean species to add to the plantings of the eighteenth century and to enhance the Italian character of the garden.

The great terrace is bounded on one side by an elegant colonnade and commands lovely views out over the orchard and the surrounding countryside. Paths wander through the Woodland and garden to the summerhouse, the cloister and the casita and amongst the water features.

Fact File

Opening Times:	2pm - 5pm Sundays April and October.
	2pm - 5pm Tuesdays - Thursdays, Saturday, Sunday and Bank Holiday Mondays, May to September, Mornings and Mondays and Fridays reserved for group visits by appointment.
Admission Rates:	Adults £4.00, Senior Citizen £3.50, Child over 10 yrs £3.50.
Group Rates:	Minimum group size: 8
	Adults £4.50, Senior Citizen £4.50, Child over 10 yrs £4.50
Facilities:	House Keeper Teas - May to August at weekends
Disabled Access:	Yes, Toilet and parking for disabled on site.
Tours/Events:	By appointment
Coach Parking:	Yes.
Length of Visit:	1 1/2 hours
Booking Contact:	Mrs Elizabeth Cartwright-Hignett
	The Peto Garden, Iford Manor, Bradford on Avon, Wiltshire BA15 2BA
	Telephone:01225 863146 Fax: 01225 862364
Website:	www.ifordmanor.co.uk
Location:	Follow brown tourist signs to Iford Manor. 7 miles south of Bath on A36 Warminster Road and 1/2 mile south of Bradford on Avon on B3109.

Please quote this guide when booking

Pound Hill is a 2 acre, garden planted in a romantic, English style. Its reputation for design and horticultural excellence is widely acknowledged and it was recently appointed as a partner garden to the Royal Horticultural Society.

The garden has been laid out as a series of individually designed rooms, in scale with the central 16th century Cotswold farmhouse. You approach the garden through an inspiring retail nursery, which has a most inviting selection of herbaceous perennials, unusual topiary and old roses. Inside the garden you first encounter a formal kitchen garden and a small rose garden planted with old roses. The main part of the garden is laid out with structure given by box hedging, yew cones in the design of deep Jekyll borders, lawn and substantial parteere. There is also a courtyard garden, a wildlife pond and avenues of white-stemmed birch and topiarized chestnuts with inspiring underplanting of spring bulbs and old roses.

Fact File

Opening Times: Plant Centre daily & Bank Holidays 10am - 5pm, closed January.
Garden daily & Bank Holidays 2pm - 5pm March - October.
Admission Rates: Adults £3.50, Senior Citizen £3.50, Child Free.
Facilities: Shop, Plant Sales, Coffee, Lunch, Tea, Restaurant, Study Mornings and RHS Events.
Disabled Access: Yes. Parking for disabled on site.
Tours/Events: Please telephone for details of special events. RHS study mornings, expert lectures, wholesale nursery open days.
Coach Parking: Yes.
Length of Visit: 2 hours
Booking Contact: Philip Stockitt
Pound Hill, West Kington, Chippendham, Wiltshire, SN14 7JG
Telephone: 01249 783880 Fax: 01249 782953
Email: info@poundhillplants.co.uk
Website: www.poundhillplants.co.uk
Location: From Bath or the M4 junction 18 follow the A46 and turn onto the A420 towards Chippenham. After 2.5 miles follow brown signs to Pound Hill.

Please quote this guide when booking

Stourhead   Wiltshire

An outstanding example of the English landscape style, this splendid garden was designed by Henry Hoare II and laid out between 1741 and 1780. Classical temples, including the Pantheon and the Temple of Apollo, are situated around the central lake at the end of a series of vistas, which change as the visitor moves around the paths and through the magnificent mature woodland with its extensive collection of trees and shrubs.

Although Stourhead has changed and developed over more than two centuries, it remains as Horace Walpole described it in the 18th century: "One of the most picturesque scenes in the world".

The Stourhead Estate extends from the edge of the Wiltshire Downs in the east to King Alfred's Tower in the west, a 160 ft folly with views across Somerset, Dorset and Wiltshire.

Fact File

Opening Times: All year, daily from 9am until 7pm, or dusk if earlier. (House open Friday - Tuesday, 18th March - 31st October 11am - 4pm).

Admission Rates: Adults £5.80, Child £3.20, National Trust Members free.

Group Rates: Minimum group size: 15, Adults £5.10, National Trust Members free.

Facilities: Visitor Centre, Shop, Plant Sales, Self Service Restaurant, Spread Eagle Inn.

Disabled Access: Yes. Toilet and parking for disabled on site. Wheelchairs on loan.

Tours/Events: Many different group packages available including lunch or refreshments. August 2005 - Around the garden with the plant hunters, Exhibition + Tours. Please ask for the Group information Guide. Walks, talks, painting, music, theatre and childrens events take place all year. For events leaflet call 01747 841152

Coach Parking: Yes.

Length of Visit: Minimum 2 hours.

Booking Contact: Georgina Mead. Stourhead Estate Office, Stourton, Nr Mere, Warminster, Wiltshire BA12 6QD Tel: 01747 841152 Fax: 01747 842005

Email: stourhead@nationaltrust.org.uk

Website: www.nationaltrust.org.uk

Location: Stourhead is in the village of Stourton, off the B3092, 3 miles north west of Mere (A303). It is 8 miles south of Frome (A361).

Please quote this guide when booking

The gardens at Wilton House have changed considerably over the years, often reflecting the styles of the day and the individual tastes of each Earl and Countess of Pembroke. In an idyllic setting the grounds are bordered by the rivers Wylye and Nadder. A mix of open parkland in the style of 'Capability' Brown and small formal gardens. The latter created by the 17th Earl who began a programme of garden development soon after succeeding to the title in 1969.

The four new gardens created are the Rose Garden, the Water Garden, the Tudor Knot Garden and the North Forecourt Garden. There are a wealth of architectural features from the earlier Renaissance and 18th century gardens. There is also a woodland walk with its collection of many interesting trees from around the world. The latest addition of the Millennium Water Feature forms a contrast to the famous Palladian Bridge.

Fact File

Opening Times: 24th March - 30th October 2005.

Admission Rates: House & Grounds (Grounds Only) Adults £9.75 (£4.50), Senior Citizen £8.00 (£4.50), Child £5.50 (£3.50).

Group Rates: Minimum group size: 15
Adults £7.00, Senior Citizen £6.50, Child £4.50.

Facilities: Visitor Centre, Gift Shop, Teas, Restaurant, Historic House and Exhibitions. Plant Sales at adjacent Garden Centre.

Disabled Access: Yes. Toilet and parking for disabled on site. Wheelchairs on loan, booking advisable.

Tours/Events: Events Programme.

Coach Parking: Yes.

Length of Visit: 4 1/2 hours - House & Grounds. 3 hours - Grounds only.

Booking Contact: Sandra Piper
Wilton House, Wilton, Salisbury, Wiltshire, SP2 0BJ
Tel: 01722 746720 Fax: 01722 744447

Email: tourism@wiltonhouse.com

Website: www.wiltonhouse.com

Location: 3 miles west of Salisbury off the A36

Please quote this guide when booking

Arley Arboretum & Gardens   Worcestershire

This jewel in Worcestershire's crown was, until two years ago, opened only occasionally to the public and is possibly the oldest privately owned Arboretum in the country. It is a haven of peace and tranquillity which overlooks the banks of the River Severn close to the picturesque village of Upper Arley. Approached through rolling parkland, entrance is made through a listed Walled Garden which contains an Italianate Garden, raised beds, orchard, herbaceous borders, ornamental fowl, picnic area and plant sales.

With planting commencing in 1820 by Lord Mountnorris, it is now a mature and majestic Arboretum with awe-inspiring trees (some of which are record breaking and includes the tallest Crimean Pine in Britain) underplanted with rhododendrons, azaleas and camellias and 1000's of spring flowering bulbs together with a delightful Magnolia Walk.

Fact File

Opening Times:	1st April - 31st October.
	Wednesday, Thursday, Friday, Saturday, Sunday & Bank Holiday Mondays 10am - 5pm.
Admission Rates:	Adults £4.00, Senior Citizens £4.00, Child £1.00
Groups Rates:	Minimum group size: 20 - £3.50.
Facilities:	Picnic Area, Plant Sales, Dogs on leads and Tea Rooms serving Hot & Cold Refreshments.
Disabled Access:	Yes. Toilet and parking for disabled on site. Wheelchairs on loan.
Tours/Events:	None.
Coach Parking:	Yes
Length of Visit:	2 hours
Booking Contact:	Nora Howells
	Arley Arboretum, Arley Estate Office, Arley, Nr Bewdley, Worcs, DY12 1XG
	Telephone: 01299 861868 or 01299 861368
Email:	info@arley-arboretum.org.uk
Website:	www.arley-arboretum.org.uk
Location:	Off the A442 - Kidderminster/Bridgnorth/Telford Road - brown signed from Shatterford on A442.

Please quote this guide when booking

Bodenham Arboretum   Worcestershire

Bodenham Arboretum has been awarded National Heritage status for the creation of a new English landscape and Arboretum, and a Centre of Excellence by the Forestry Authority who described it as "a showpiece woodland rich in habitats for wild flowers, water-fowl and other birds".

Over 2700 species of trees and shrubs landscaped within 156 acres, incorporating a working farm, four miles of paths through dells, glades, lakes, pools and fields where sheep and cattle graze and rare breeds of poultry roam. Daffodils and primroses in March and April, bluebells in May, the laburnum tunnel from mid May to mid June and the vibrant colours in Autumn are special attractions for visitors.

The unique underground visitors centre with its restaurant overlooking the big pool, won the CLA President award for the best new rural building in England and Wales 1998/99.

Fact File

Opening Times: Open daily: 11am - 5pm March - Christmas
Closed: Mon & Tues, except in May, June, October and Bank Holidays
Admission Rates: Adults £5.00, Child £2.00 (5-16 yrs) Wheelchair users £2.00
Groups Rates: Minimum group size 25, prior booking is essential.
Adults £4.50, Child £2.00 (no charge for teachers in school parties)
Facilities: Visitor Centre, Restaurant, Shop, Plant Sales. Jan & Feb weekdays - no restaurant facilities.
Disabled Access: Yes. Visitor Centre fully accesible. Arboretum limited access.
Toilet and parking for disabled on site.
Tours/Events: Guided tours by arrangement £25 1 - 1 1/2 hours.
Spring Plant Fair, Autumn Craft Fair. Please ring for details.
Coach Parking: Yes
Length of Visit: 2 hours - all day.
Booking Contact: James Binnian.
Bodenham Arboretum, Wolverley, Kidderminster, DY11 5SY
Telephone: 01562 852444 Fax: 01562 852777
Email: None
Website: www.bodenham-arboretum.co.uk
Location: Map reference SO 8081. Brown signs from Wolverley Church Island along B4189 (2 miles).

Please quote this guide when booking

This lovely 30 acre garden is owned by the Berkeley family, whose other home is historic 12th Century Berkeley Castle in Gloucestershire.

At Spetchley you will find most aspects of gardening, the formal and informal, woodland and herbaceous. A Garden full of secrets, every corner reveals some new vista, some new treasure of the plant world, whether it be tree, shrub or plant. The exuberant planting and the peaceful walks make this an oasis of peace and quiet. Many of the vast collection of plants are rarely found outside the major botanical gardens. The wonderful display of spring bulbs in April and May, together with flowering trees and shrubs, are followed in June and July by the large selection of roses, whilst July, August and September reveal the great herbaceous borders in all their glory. This is indeed a garden for all seasons.

Fact File

Opening Times: 25th March - 30th September. Tuesday - Friday 11am - 6pm, Sundays 2pm - 6pm, Bank Holiday Mondays 11am - 6pm. Closed all Saturdays and all other Mondays. Last admissions on all opening days 4pm.

Admission Rates: Adults £5.00, Senior Citizen £5.00, Child £2.00,

Group Rates: Minimum group size: 25
Adults £4.50, Senior Citizen £4.50, Child £1.90.

Facilities: Tea Room

Disabled Access: Partial. Parking for disabled on site. Booking necessary for parties. (Access restricted, please telephone contact details below for advice).

Tours/Events: Specialist Plant Fair 24th April 2005. Concert Sat 2nd July.

Coach Parking: Yes.

Length of Visit: 2 hours minimum.

Booking Contact: Berkeley Estate Office, Ham, Berkeley, Gloucestershire GL13 9QL.
Tel: 01453 810303 Fax: 01453 511915

Email: hb@spetchleygardens.co.uk

Website: www.spetchleygardens.co.uk

Location: 2 miles east of Worcester on A44, leave M5 at either junctions 6 or 7

Please quote this guide when booking

Bramham Park is the stunning family home of the Lane Fox family, direct descendents of Robert Benson, the founder of Bramham over 300 years ago. The gardens cover some 66 acres and with the Pleasure Grounds extend to over 100 acres.

Inspiration for the design of the garden at Bramham was French and formal, but the manner in which it was adapted to the national landscape is relaxed and entirely English. It is completely original and few other parks of this period survive; none on the scale and complexity of Bramham.

Bramham is a garden of walks and vistas, architectural features and reflecting water. A broad vista stretches away at an angle from the house and a number of other allees have focal points.

The house, gardens and surrounding parkland make an ideal venue for events, private dinners, corporate entertaining, product launches and filming.

Fact File

Opening Times: 1st April - 30th September 2005, 11.30am - 4.30pm Daily.
Closed 6th-12th June Inc. for Bramham International Horse Trials
Closed 15th August - 2nd September Inc. 2005 for Leeds Festival.

Admission Rates: Adults £4.00, Senior Citizen £2.00, Child 5 - 16yrs £2.00 (under 5's Free).

Groups Rate: House only open for pre-booked morning visits - 10 or more, £10.00 per person.
Gardens - 20 or more 15% discount.

Facilities: Small Tea Room serving hot drinks, Home-made Cakes, Sweets, Crisps etc.

Disabled Access: Yes. Toilet and parking for disabled on site.

Tours/Events: None

Coach Parking: Yes

Length of Visit: 2 - 3 hours

Booking Contact: Judy Fisk
Bramham Park, Bramham, Wetherby, West Yorkshire, LS23 6ND
Telephone: 01937 846000 Fax: 01937 846007

Email: judy.fisk@bramhampark.co.uk

Website: www.bramhampark.co.uk.

Location: Just off the A1, 5 miles from Wetherby 7 miles from Leeds, 14 miles from York.

Please quote this guide when booking

Fountains Abbey & Studley Royal Water Garden   Yorkshire

One of the most remarkable sites in Europe, sheltered in a secluded valley, Fountains Abbey and Studley Royal, a World Heritage Site, encompasses the spectacular remains of a 12th century Cistercian abbey with one of the finest surviving monastic watermills in Britain, an Elizabethan mansion, and one of the best surviving examples of a Georgian green water garden. Elegant ornamental lakes, avenues, temples and cascades provide a succession of unforgettable eye-catching vistas in an atmosphere of peace and tranquillity. St Mary's Church, built by William Burges in the 19th century, provides a dramatic focal point to the medieval Deer park with over 500 Deer.

Small museum near to the Abbey. Exhibitions in Fountains Hall, Swanley Grange and the Mill.

Fact File

Opening Times: March - October 10am - 5pm, November - February 10am - 4pm.
Closed Fridays in November - January and closed 24th and 25th December.

Admission Rates: Adults £5.50, Senior Citizen £5.50, Child £3.00, NT/EH Members Free, Family's £15.00.

Groups Rates: Minimum group size: 31 plus (Also do a 15 -30 group rate - please call for details)
Adults £4.50, Senior Citizen £4.50, Child £2.20, NT/EH Members Free.

Facilities: Visitor Centre, Shop, Tea Room, Restaurant, Kiosk.

Disabled Access: Yes. Toilet and parking for disabled on site. Wheelchairs on loan, booking necessary.

Tours/Events: Guided Tours for groups, must be pre booked, telephone 01765 643197.
Annual events programme, please enquire for details.

Coach Parking: Yes

Length of Visit: 1 1/2 hours minimum.

Booking Contact: Fountains Abbey, Ripon, Yorkshire, HG4 3DY
Telephone: 01765 608888   Fax: 01765 601002

Email: fountainsenquiries@nationaltrust.org.uk

Website: www.fountainsabbey.org.uk

Location: 4 miles west of Ripon of B6265 to Pateley Bridge, signposted from A1, 10 miles north of Harrogate A61.

Please quote this guide when booking

One of Yorkshire's most relaxing yet inspiring locations, situated on the outskirts of the spa town of Harrogate. As the newest RHS garden, Harlow Carr has seen many exciting developments during the last twelve months, whilst still retaining its uniquely tranquil and welcoming atmosphere. Probably the most spectacular change is the opening of the *Gardens through Time* - seven fascinating historical gardens created to mark the bicentenary of the RHS in 2004, and recently televised on BBC2.

A beautiful and peaceful garden draws inspiration from the local scenery and stretches across 58 acres. Highlights include: streamside garden, flower and vegetable trials; contemporary grass border; scented herb and foliage gardens; woodland, arboretum and wildflower meadow. Masses of fascinating events take place throughout the year including outdoor theatre, festivals and children's activities. An extensive range of over 70 gardening & horticulture workshops is also available.

Fact File

Opening Times: 9.30am - 6pm (4pm Nov - Feb incl.) with last entry 1 hour before closing.
Admission Rates: Adults £5.50, Child (6-16yrs) £1.50 (under 6 Free).
Groups Rates: Minimum group size 10, Adults £4.50.
Facilities: Largest Gardening Bookshop in the north, Gift Shop, Bettys Garden Cafe, Plant Centre, Museum of Gardening.
Disabled Access: Yes. Toilet and parking for disabled on site. Wheelchairs on loan, booking necessary.
Tours/Events: A full programme of events is available from the gardens.
Coach Parking: Yes
Length of Visit: 1 - 2 hours
Booking Contact: Moira Malcolm
RHS Garden Harlow Carr, Crag Lane, Harrogate, HG3 1QB
Tel: 01423 565418 Fax: 01423 530663
Email: admin-harlowcarr@rhs.org.uk
Website: www.rhs.org.uk
Location: Take the B6162 Otley Road out of Harrogate towards Beckwithshaw. Harlow Carr is 1.5 miles on the right.

Please quote this guide when booking

Newby Hall was built between 1691-1695, shortly afterwards the owner, Sir Edward Blackett, commissioned Peter Aram to lay out formal gardens in keeping with the period. Very little of Aram's layout for Newby remains today and the present design is largely attributable to the present owner's grandfather, the late Major Edward Compton, who inherited in 1921. Influenced by Lawrence Johnston's Hidcote Manor in Gloucestershire, he created a main axis for the garden running from the south front of the house down to the River Ure. The axis consisted of double herbaceous borders flanked by yew hedges. Either side of the borders are numerous compartmented gardens such as the Rose Garden, the Autumn Garden, the Rock Garden, the Laburnum pergola walk, a Water Garden and even a Tropical Garden here in North Yorkshire - truly a 'Garden for all Seasons'. Newby also holds the National Collection of CORNUS.

Fact File

Opening Times: 25th March - End of Sptember, 11am - 5.30pm, Tuesday - Sunday & Bank Holidays.
Admission Rates: (2004 Rates).
Adults £6.30, Senior Citizen £5.30, Child £4.80.
Groups Rates: Minimum group size 15
Adults £5.30, Senior Citizen £5.30, Child £4.30
Facilities: Visitor Centre, Shop, Plant Sales, Teas, Restaurant.
Disabled Access: Yes. Toilet and parking for disabled on site. Wheelchairs on loan, booking necessary.
Tours/Events: Tours on request with pre-booking essential.
Coach Parking: Yes
Length of Visit: 2 hours minimum
Booking Contact: Rosemary Triffit
Newby Hall, Ripon, North Yorkshire, HG4 5AE
Tel: 01423 322583 Fax: 01423 324452
Email: info@newbyhall.com
Website: www.newbyhall.com
Location: 2 miles from A1M at Ripon exit - junction 48.

Please quote this guide when booking

These substantial walled gardens and wooded pleasure grounds, recently restored and much improved, are well worth visiting in all seasons: massive herbaceous borders, Victorian Kitchen garden with rare vegetable collection, the National Hyacinth Collection, herb and shade borders, extensive hothouses and thousands of snowdrops, bluebells, daffodils and narcissi. A stroll around the lake takes you through the deer park, where fallow deer graze beneath the boughs of living oak trees, now believed to be over a thousand years old. This walk also offers the best views of the 14th century castle.

Guided tours of the castle give you a chance to view the civil war armour, secret priests hiding hole and splendid furnishings. On site facilities include ample free parking, wc's (including disabled), tea room, historic inn with beer garden and gift shop selling plants.

Fact File

Opening Times: Daily - Throughout the year 9am - 5pm (dusk in the winter months).

Admission Rates: Adults £4.00, Senior Citizen £3.50, Child £2.50. (under 5 yrs Free)

Groups Rates: Minimum group size 15 people
Adults £3.50, Senior Citizen £3.50, Child £2.50.

Facilities: Gift Shop, Plant Sales, Tea Rooms, Restaurant.

Disabled Access: Yes. Toilet and parking for disabled on site. Wheelchairs on loan, booking necessary.

Tours/Events: Guided tours of gardens by prior arrangement only.

Coach Parking: Yes

Booking Contact: Mrs Wendy McNae
Ripley Castle Gardens, Ripley, Nr Harrogate, North Yorkshire, HG3 3AY
Telephone: 01423 770152 Fax: 01423 771745

Email: groups@ripleycastle.co.uk

Website: www.ripleycastle.co.uk

Location: Three miles north of Harrogate on the A61.

Please quote this guide when booking

Sausmarez Manor - Subtropical Gardens & Art Park   Guernsey

Set around two small lakes in an ancient wood is a garden which has been crammed with the unusual and rare, to give an exotic feel. It is strewn with plants from many parts of the world, particularly the sub-tropics and the Mediterranean, which survive in Guernsey's mellow maritime climate.

Collections of yuccas, ferns, camellias (over 300), bamboos, hebes, bananas, echiums, lilies, palm trees, fuchsias, as well as hydrangeas, hostas, azaleas, pittosporums, clematis, rhododendrons, cyclamens, impatiens, giant grasses etc. - all jostle with indigenous wild flowers. No pesticides are used so wildlife flourishes. Also here is the Art park, showing around 200 pieces of sculpture by about 90 British, European, African, American and local artists, all for sale.

Fact File

Opening Times: February to Mid December.
Admission Rates: Adults £4.50, Senior Citizen £3.50, Child £3.50.
Groups Rates: Minimum group size: 10
Adults £4.00, Senior Citizen £3.00, Child £3.00.
Facilities: Gift Shop, Plant Sales, Teas, Sculpture Park, Pitch and Putt course.
Historic House open to the public and Dolls House collection.
Disabled Access: Partial, Parking for disabled on site.
Tours/Events: Giant Plant sale - May Bank Holiday.
Coach Parking: Yes
Length of Visit: 1 hour for garden, 4 hours for all things of interest.
Booking Contact: Peter De Sausmarez
Sausmarez Manor, St Martin, Guernsey, GY4 6SG.
Telephone: 01481 235571 Fax: 01481 235572
Email: sausmarezmanor@cwgsy.net
Website: www.artparks.co.uk
Location: 1 mile south of St Peterport.

Please quote this guide when booking

Scotland

"The quality of light surpasses all other places ... as the mist lessens the loch glistens whilst the gorse and heather burst into flame. Even the funereal peat softens, as if in response to the deepening red of the pine".

'On the Western Isle' E.B. Hamilton

Scottish gardens are unique. They may contain (in some instances) similar plants and architecture to their English cousins but there the similarity ends. The rich acid soils, abundance of water and clarity of air combine to create plants of great vigour and stunning vistas - both within the garden and to the borrowed landscape beyond. From Castle Kennedy in the south to Armadale Castle on the Isle of Skye this book provides a choice selection of Scotland's finest gardens.

Opposite: Torosay Castle and Gardens (page 165)

Armadale Castle Gardens & Museum of the Isles   Isle of Skye

Armadale Castle Gardens & Museum of the Isles has a spectacular setting within the Sleat Peninsula of the Isle of Skye called the 'Garden of Skye'.

The forty acre Garden is set around the ruins of Armadale Castle. The warm, generally frost free climate of the west coast of Scotland - a result of the Gulf Stream - allows these sheltered gardens, dating back to the 17th Century, to flourish.

Wander over the expanses of lawn leading from the ruined Armadale Castle to viewpoints overlooking the hills of Knoydart. Terraced walks and landscaped ponds contrasting with wildflower meadows bring the natural and formal side by side. The Nature Trails provide another dimension to this garden experience. In May during the bluebell season, a carpet of blue around the Arboretum creates a visual and fragrance sensation that is so prevalent around the gardens at that time of year.

Fact File

Opening Times: 9.30am - 5.00pm (last entry 5pm), 7 days April to October (incl).
Admission Rates: Adults £4.80, Senior Citizen £3.50, Child £3.50, Family £14.00.
Groups Rates: Minimum group size: 8
Adults £3.20, Senior Citizen £3.20, Child £3.20.
Facilities: Restaurant, Shops, Garden Shop, Museum, 40 Acre Garden with Ponds, Lawns, Wildflower Meadows, Nature Trails.
Disabled Access: Yes, Toilet and Parking for disabled on site. Electric Wheelchairs on loan, booking necessary.
Tours/Events: Guided walks on request.
Coach Parking: Yes
Length of Visit: 2 hours
Booking Contact: Mags MacDonald
Armadale Castle, Armadale, Sleat, Isle of Skye, IV45 8RS
Telephone: 01471 844305 Fax: 01471 844275
Email: office@clandonald.com
Website: www.clandonald.com
Location: 2 minutes from Armadale/Mallaig Ferry. 20 miles from Skyebridge on A851.

Please quote this guide when booking

There has been a garden on this site for 200 years, but the present garden was started by the owner's grandparents in the 1920's and reshaped by his uncle over the last 20 years.

Three acres of plantsmen's garden are well laid out within a walled enclosure and demonstrate the potential of an exposed hillside site with a northerly aspect. Astounding views over the Tay Valley are matched by the garden's own interesting features, including peat walks and a stream garden. There are masses of fine bulbs in spring and good autumn colour. Gentians, meconopsis, ericaceous plants and celmisias do well on this soil. The Walled garden contains a collection of old and modern shrub roses and rambling roses.

Fact File

Opening Times: April - October, Daily 10am - 6pm
Admission Rates: Adults £3.00, (2004 prices) Child Free.
Facilities: Teas, Toilet Facilities, Plants for Sale.
Disabled Access: Partial.
Tours/Events: None
Coach Parking: Please call for details.
Booking Contact: R A Price
Bolfracks Estate Office, Aberfeldy, Perthshire, PH15 2EX
Telephone: 01887 820344 Fax: 01887 829522
Email: infor@bolfracks.fsnet.co.uk
Website: None
Location: 2 miles west of Aberfeldy on A827 towards Loch Tay.

Please quote this guide when booking

A beautiful landscaped garden extending to 75 acres set between two large freshwater lochs. The gardens are famous for their collection of trees and rhododendrons from around the world.

The grounds were extensively landscaped in the 18th century laid out with terraces and avenues. The plant collections include specimens provided by Joseph Hooker and probably the oldest avenue of Monkey Puzzle trees.

Fact File

Opening Times:	Easter - 30th September, seven days a week, 10am- 5pm.
Admission Rates:	Adults £4.00, Senior Citizen £3.00, Child £1.00
Groups Rates:	Minimum group size 20
	10% discount on normal admission rates.
Facilities:	Tea Shop, Plant sales.
Disabled Access:	Limited. Toilet and parking for disabled on site.
Tours/Events:	None.
Coach Parking:	Yes
Length of Visit:	1 - 4 hours
Booking Contact:	Castle Kennedy Gardens, Stair Estates, Rephad, Stanraer, Dumfries & Galloway, DG9 8BX
	Gardens Tel: 01581 400225 Telephone: 01776 702024 Fax: 01776 706248
Email:	info@castlekennedygardens.co.uk
Website:	www.castlekennedygardens.co.uk
Location:	Approximately 5 miles east of Stranraer on A75.

Please quote this guide when booking

Cherrybank Garden is home to the Bell's National Heather Collection; A Superb 7 acre site housing some 50,000 plants with over 900 varieties of Heather.

The visitor centre includes something for all the family with a dedicated area for children's play, an aviary and the Bell's putting green.

The 'Pride of Perth Exhibition' illustrates the full city's story from medieval times to present day incurring it's association with Scottish kings and important battles.

Relax and unwind in the garden terrace cafe and experience our freshly prepared snacks and homebaking or sample our collection of rare single malts in the Whisky shop. Round off your visit by browsing through our gift shop with a wide range of Scottish produce, plants arts and crafts.

Fact File

Opening Times:	Mar - Oct, (Mon - Sat 10 - 5, Sun 12 - 5), Nov - Dec (Mon- Sat 10 - 4, Sun 12 - 4) Jan - Feb (Thurs - Sat 10 - 4, Sun 12 - 4).
Admission Rates:	Adults £3.00, Senior Citizen £2.70, Child Free under 16.
Group Rates:	Minimum group size: 10 Adults £2.70, Senior Citizen £ 2.70, Child Free under 16.
Facilities:	Visitor Centre, Gift Shop, Plant Sales, Cafe Serving Hot & Cold Snacks, Whisky Sales.
Disabled Access:	Yes. Toilet and parking for disabled on site. Wheelchairs on loan, booking advisable.
Tours/Events:	Please call for details.
Coach Parking:	No, although usually space in car park.
Length of Visit:	1 1/2 - 2 hours
Booking Contact:	The Visitor Centre Cherrybank Gardens, Necessity Brae, Perth, PN2 0PF. Telephone: 01738 472818 Fax: 01738 472805
Email:	info@thecalyx.co.uk
Website:	www.thecalyx.co.uk
Location:	Main entrance on Necessity Brae, just off A93 Glasgow Road, between Perth Park & Ride, (Broxden) and city centres.

Please quote this guide when booking

The garden lies hidden under the lee of Hunterheck Hill; the Craigieburn cascades down through its deep wooded gorge. In Craigieburn's five acres of garden you will find an extraordinary range of plants. The climate and terrain are reminiscent of Nepal, and Himalayan plants thrive in abundance. Blue poppies, giant lilies, squadrons of candelabra primulas, bizarre arisaemas fill the glades.

Elsewhere, human artifice is more evident. This is a new garden made on a old base: the lines of beech trees and old hollies were planted in 1796. Two eighty yard double borders in a classic style are filled with an eclectic range of bulbs, herbaceous plants and shrubs. It is a highly personal garden, overflowing with plants that Janet Wheatcroft and gardener Datenji Sherpa prize.

Every year they propagate for the garden, and in the little nursery the same desirable plants are for sale.

Fact File

Opening Times: 25th March - 30th October, Friday - Sunday and all Bank Holidays, other times by appointment only.

Admission Rates: Adults £2.00, Senior Citizen £2.00, Child Free (under 12)

Groups Rates: Minimum group size: 15
Adults £1.50, Senior Citizen £1.50, Child Free (under 12)

Facilities: Plant Sales, Dogs welcome.

Disabled Access: No

Tours/Events: Guided tours by arrangement.

Coach Parking: No

Length of Visit: 1 1/2 - 2 hours

Booking Contact: Andrew Wheatcroft
Craigieburn House, By Moffat, Dumfriesshire, Scotland, DG10 9LF.
Telephone: 01683 221250 Fax: 01683 221250 (non Automatic).

Email: ajmw1@aol.con

Website: None

Location: Three miles from M74, on A708 Moffat to Selkirk road, 2 miles from Moffat. Entrance beside Victorian Gate Lodge, yellow sign for Craigieburn Garden.

Please quote this guide when booking

There is no clue as to what awaits as one drives up a mile-long avenue, closely lined with beech trees. The castle sits on a rocky outcrop and is everything you would expect of an ancient Scottish Fortress. Huge walls, a massive keep and spiralling turrets.

On crossing the castle courtyard the gardens are revealed. Standing at the top of a flight of stairs that lead down into the gardens themselves, it is possible to see the full glory of the gardens. Intricate parterres are lined with low box hedges. They depict family crests, contained within a St Andrew's cross. Gravel paths sit alongside neatly clipped yew hedges.

This is a formal Italianate garden sitting amidst the splendour of Scotland's rolling countryside. It is the perfect way to spend a relaxing afternoon walking amongst the plants, exploring the greenhouses or sitting on a bench, soaking up the atmosphere.

Fact File

Opening Times:	Easter Weekend then daily 1st May - October 1pm - 6pm.
Admission Rates:	Adults £4.00, Senior Citizen £3.00, Child £1.50
Groups Rates:	Minimum group size: 20 plus 10% discount on normal admission rates.
Facilities:	Lavatories. Guide book, postcards, soft drinks.
Disabled Access:	Partial. Toilet and parking for disabled on site.
Tours/Events:	Private morning/early evening visits for groups. Guided tours with horticultural or architectural theme. Option to visit the 15th century Tower. (all by arrangement)
Coach Parking:	Yes
Length of Visit:	Minimum 1 hour.
Booking Contact:	Joe Buchanan Drummond Castle Gardens, Muthill, Crieff, Perthshire, PH5 2AA Telephone: 01764 681257 Fax: 01764 681550
Email:	thegardens@drummondcastle.co.uk
Website:	www.drummondcastlegardens.co.uk
Location:	2 miles south of Crieff off the A822.

Please quote this guide when booking

Hercules Garden & Blair Castle   Perthshire

Hercules Garden is a walled garden of ten acres, over looked by a fine statue of Hercules by John Cheere, placed on a rise in a shrub walk running east from Blair Castle, the ancestral home of the Dukes of Atholl. It was the 2nd Duke who landscaped the grounds in the mid 18th century, his scheme evolved to create two ponds in a large walled garden designed in the 'Ferme Ornee' manner-fruit and vegetables grown among ornamental planting schemes and sweet smelling shrubs.

Today the garden contains a large collection of fruit trees, a terrace over 300 meters long flanked by herbaceous borders, a variety of beds for vegetables, herbs, cut flowers, shade loving plants, roses and annuals. The layout is based on the 2nd Duke's design and includes some of the original, heather thatched huts for the nesting birds and a restored folly, housing a display about the restoration of the garden.

Fact File

Opening Times: 9.30am - 4.30pm last entry.
Admission Rates: Grounds & Garden: Adults £2.20, Senior Citizen £2.20, Children £1.10.
Group Rates: As Above.
Facilities: Shop, Teas, Restaurant, Castle (5 Star historic Home).
Disabled Access: Yes. Toilet & parking for disabled on site. Wheelchairs on loan, booking necessary.
Tours/Events: Please call for details or visit website.
Coach Parking: Yes
Length of Visit: Approx 2 hours
Booking Contact: Admin Office
Blair Castle, Blair Atholl, Pitlochry, Perthshire PH18 5TL
Telephone 01796 481207 Fax: 01796 481487
Email: office@blair-castle.co.uk
Website: www.blair-castle.co.uk
Location: Off A9 Blair Atholl on Perth/Inverness Road (35mins Perth). 1 1/2 hours Edinburgh.

Please quote this guide when booking

Torosay Castle and Gardens

Isle of Mull

Torosay Castle, completed in 1858 in the Scottish Baronial style by the eminent architect David Bryce, is one of the finer examples of his work, resulting in a combination of elegance and informality, grandeur and homeliness.

A unique combination of formal terraces and dramatic West Highland scenery makes Torosay a spectacular setting, which, together with a mild climate results in superb specimens of rare, unusual and beautiful plants.

A large collection of Statuary and many niche gardens makes Torosay a joy to explore and provides many peaceful corners in which to relax.

Fact File

Opening Times:	House: 25th March - 31st October, 10.30am - 5pm.
	Gardens: Open all year.
Admission Rates:	Adults £5.50, Concessions £5.00, Child £2.25.
Group Rates:	Minimum group size: 10
	Adults £5.00, Concessions £5.00, Child £2.00.
Facilities:	Shop, Plant Sales, Children's Play Area, Tea Room, Holiday Cottages, Parking on site.
Disabled Access:	Yes to gardens only. Toilet and parking for disabled on site.
Tours/Events:	Tours available to groups by arrangement at a cost of £7 per person.
	Concerts, plays etc advertised separately.
Coach Parking:	Yes
Length of Visit:	2 hours minimum.
Booking Contact:	Mr James/Carol Casey.
	Torosay Castle, Craignure, Isle of Mull PA65 6AY
	Telephone: 01680 812421 Fax: 01680 812470
Email:	torosay@aol.com
Website:	www.torosay.com
Location:	1 1/2 miles from Craignure (ferry terminal) on A849/on foot by forest walk or by narrow gauge railway.

Please quote this guide when booking

Wales

*"It is warming indeed to see the avenues that I then planted
growing so flourishingly and the whole place maturing
in ever increasing beauty".*

Clough Williams-Ellis

From Cardiff Bay to the mountains of Snowdonia, Wales is a
country of contrasts. This is clearly portrayed by the gardens
in this book. Here you will find gardens of yesterday and
gardens of tomorrow. From the fifteenth century beginnings
of Aberglasney to the twenty-first century steel and glass
structures of Middleton, there are inspirational gardens in
Wales for us all to enjoy.

Opposite: Portmeirion (page 175)

Aberglasney Gardens   Carmarthenshire

Aberglasney is one of the Country's most exciting garden restoration projects. The Gardens have wonderful horticultural qualities and a mysterious history. Within the nine acres of garden are six different garden spaces including three walled gardens. At its heart is a unique and fully restored Elizabethan/Jacobean cloister garden and a parapet walk, which is the only example that survives in the UK. The Garden already contains a magnificent collection of rare and unusual plants which are seldom seen elsewhere in the country.

The House and Garden will continually be improved over the years, the result will be a world renowned Garden set in the beautiful landscape of the Tywi Valley. There is a Cafe in the grounds, which serves delectable light lunches and snacks. In the summer, tea can be taken on the terrace overlooking the Pool Garden. There is also a new shop and plant sales area, which can be visited without admission to the garden.

Fact File

Opening Times: Summer: 10am - 6pm (last entry at 5pm).
Winter: 10.30am - 4pm.

Admission Rates: Adults £6.00, Senior Citizen £5.00, Child £3.00

Groups Rates: Minimum group size 10
Adults £5.50, Senior Citizen £4.50, Child £3.00

Facilities: Shop, Plant Sales, Cafe.

Disabled Access: Yes. Toilet and parking for disabled on site. Wheelchairs on loan, booking necessary.

Tours/Events: Guided tours at 11.30am and 2.30pm.

Coach Parking: Yes

Length of Visit: 2 - 4 hours

Booking Contact: Bookings Department.
Aberglasney Gardens, Llangathen, Carmarthenshire, SA32 8QH
Telephone: 01558 668998   Fax: 01558 668998

Email: info@aberglasney.org.uk

Website: www.aberglasney.org

Location: Four miles outside Llandeilo of the A40.

Please quote this guide when booking

Bodnant Garden is one of the finest gardens in the country not only known for its magnificent collections of rhododendrons, camellias and magnolias but also for its idyllic setting above the River Conwy with extensive views of the Snowdonia range.

Visit in early Spring (March and April) and be rewarded by the sight of carpets of golden daffodils and other spring bulbs, as well as the beautiful blooms of the magnolias, camellias and flowering cherries. The spectacular rhododendrons and azaleas will delight from mid April until late May, whilst the famous original Laburnum Arch is an overwhelming mass of yellow blooms from mid-May to mid-June. The herbaceous borders, roses, hydrangeas, clematis and water lilies flower from the middle of June until September.

All these, together with the outstanding October autumn colours make Bodnant truly a garden and offers interest for all the seasons.

Fact File

Opening Times:	12th March - 30th Oct 2005
Admission Rates:	Adults £5.50, Child £2.75 (5-16yrs)
Groups Rates:	Minimum group size 20.
	Adults £5.00, Child £2.75.
Facilities:	Tearoom, Car & Coach Park, Plant & Gift Centre.
Disabled Access:	Yes. Toilet and parking for disabled on site. Wheelchairs on loan.
Tours/Events:	Phone for details
Coach Parking:	Yes
Length of Visit:	2 hours +
Booking Contact:	Ann Harvey
	Bodnant Garden, Tal Y cafn, Nr Colwyn Bay, Conwy, LL28 5RC
	Telephone: 01492 650460 Fax: 01492 650448
Email:	office@bodnantgarden.co.uk
Website:	www.bodnantgarden.co.uk
Location:	8 miles south of Llandudno and Colwyn Bay just off A470, signposted from the A55, exit at junction 19.

Please quote this guide when booking

Dyffryn Gardens   Vale of Glamorgan

Set in the heart of the Vale of Glamorgan countryside, this exceptional example of Edwardian garden design is currently being restored with assistance from the Heritage Lottery Fund. Designed by Thomas Mawson for the avid plant collector Reginald Cory, this unique collaboration has resulted in splendid Great Lawns, intimate garden rooms and an arboretum of rare and unusual trees from around the world.

Throughout the restoration the gardens remain open to the public with only sections of the 55 acres of designed landscape closed during the works. Restoration completed in recent years include the Pompeiian Garden, Herbaceous Border, Panel Garden, Reflecting Pool, Heather Garden and Fernery.

Ongoing works are focusing on improving access for all visitors, the glasshouse and Walled Kitchen Garden. Enjoy a relaxing stroll or come and see one of the many events taking place throughout the summer.

Fact File

Opening Times: April (or Easter) to September 10am - 6pm, October 10am - 5pm, November - March 10am - 4pm, 7 days a week.

Admission Rates: Adults £3.50, Family (2 Adults & 2 Conc.) £7.00, Conc. £2.50, Disabled £2.00, Carers Free.

Groups Rates: Minimum group size: 15 - Adults £3.00

Facilities: Visitor Centre, Shop, Tea Room, Plant Sales.

Disabled Access: Yes. Toilet and parking for disabled on site. Wheelchairs on loan, booking preferable.

Tours/Events: Tours monthly with Head Gardener no additional charge, by arrangement - Charge £1 PP. Varied programme of events from Easter to October.

Coach Parking: Yes

Length of Visit: 2 - 3 hours

Booking Contact: Mrs Deborah Kerslake
Dyffryn Gardens, St Nicholas, Vale of Glamorgan, CF5 6SU
Telephone: 029 20593328   Fax: 029 20591966

Email: dkerslake@valeofglamorgan.gov.uk

Website: www.dyffryngardens.org.uk

Location: Exit M4 at J33 to A4232 (signposted Barry). At roundabout take 1st exit (A4232). At junction with A48/A4050 exit the A4232 at Culverhouse Cross - Take 4th exit A48 (signposted Cowbridge). Turn left at lights in St Nicholas Village. Dyffryn is on right, one and a half miles.

Please quote this guide when booking

Glansevern Hall Garden Powys

Glansevern Hall was built, in Greek Revival style, by Sir Arthur Davies Owen at the turn of the 18th/19th Century.

It looks down on the River Severn from an enclosure of gardens set in wider parkland. Near the house are fine lawns studded with herbaceous and rose beds and a wide border backed by brick walls. A Victorian orangery and a large fountain face each other across the lawns. The large walled garden has been ingeniously divided into compartments separated by hornbeam hedges and ornamental ironwork. There is a rock garden of exceptional size, built of limestone and tufa, which creates a walk-through grotto. A little further afield, woodland walks are laid out around the 4 acre lake and pass through a water garden which, especially in May and June, presents a riot of growth and colour.

Glanservern is noted for its collection of unusual trees.

Fact File

Opening Times:	May - September. Thursday, Friday, Saturday & Bank Holiday Mondays, 12noon - 6pm. Group on any other day, booking necessary.
Admission Rates:	Adults £3.50, Senior Citizen £3.00, Child Free
Facilities:	Tea Room & Light Lunches (all Home-made), Plant Sales, Art Gallery.
Disabled Access:	Yes. Toilet and parking for disabled on site.
Tours/Events:	Guided walk indentifying the large number of unusual trees.
Coach Parking:	Yes
Length of Visit:	1 1/2 hours
Booking Contact:	Neville Thomas
	Glanservern Hall Gardens, Berriew, Welshpool, Powys, SY21 8AH
	Telephone: 01686 640200 Fax: 01686 640829
Email:	glansevern@ukonline.co.uk
Website:	www.glansevern.co.uk
Location:	Signposted at Berriew on A483 between Welshpool and Newtown, North Powys, 4 miles S W of Powys Castle.

Please quote this guide when booking

The gardens are perhaps the Museum's best-kept secret. From the formal gardens of the upper classes to the carefully recreated cottage gardens that provided food for working families, the gardens provide a real insight into the lives of Welsh people throughout history.

The formal gardens surrounding St Fagans Castle were once the sanctuary of the Earl of Plymouth and his family, who used the house as their summer home. The gardens are approached via a tree-lined walk and include the exquisite Rosery with its many rare and fragrant roses, the serene Italian Garden, and the elegant parterre and castle terraces.

The gardens of the re-erected houses show horticultural development from the 16th century onwards. These gardens demonstrate the social class of the buildings' inhabitants, using historically-correct plants and gardening techniques to show the age and original locality of the buildings to which they belong.

Fact File

Opening Times: Open 7 days a week 10am - 5pm, including most Public Holidays (Excluding 24-26 December, 1st January).

Admission Rates: Free Admission For All.

Group Rates: Minimum group size: 20 + (Please telephone before visiting)

Facilities: Gift Shops, Restaurant and coffee shops, Play Area, Info Desk. Toilets.

Disabled Access: Partial. Toilet and parking for disabled on site. Wheelchair on loan.

Tours/Events: Regular Events Programme.

Coach Parking: Yes

Length of Visit: 2 - 3 hours

Booking Contact: Kathryn Jenkins
Museum of Welsh Life, St Fagans, Cardiff, CF5 6XB
Telephone: 029 2057 3174 Fax: 029 2057 3126

Email: post@nmgw.ac.uk

Website: www.nmgw.ac.uk/nm1

Location: The Museum of Welsh Life is located 4 miles west of Cardiff City centre. The museum is sign-posted from junction 33 of the M4 Motorway, with direct access from the A4232.

Please quote this guide when booking

Four years after opening this remarkable 21st century botanic garden is blossoming into one of the most beautiful and stimulating gardens in the UK. Like all young things its unique character develops every year offering an unrivalled chance to see an international gem in the making.

Nested in the stunning beautiful Tywi Valley its 568 acres of lovely themed gardens, rolling regency parkland and secluded woodlands are an inspired blend on the past and future. While historic features are being proudly restored endangered Mediterranean plants are carefully conserved and displayed in the awe-inspiring Great Glasshouse.

The recently restored double walled garden is brimming with dazzling displays of the family tree of flowering plants. A new tropical house will open in 2005 adding to the many other delights which include Europe's largest herbaceous border, award winning Japanese Garden, Boulder Garden, restored lakes and cascades, interative exhibitions including a 19th century restored apothecary, children activities and discovery areas and so much more. Add to this a restaurant, shop and plant centre and you have a perfect day for all the family.

Fact File

Opening Times:	10am - 6pm British summer time. 10am - 4.30pm British winter time. (Closed Christmas Day).
Admission Rates:	Adults £7.00, Senior Citizen £5.00, Child £2.00 (5-15)
	Family (2 adults, 4 children) £16.00, Under 5's free.
Groups Rates:	Minimum group size 10
	Adults £6.00, Senior Citizen £4.00, Child £1.50
Facilities:	Visitor Centre, Shop, Restaurant, Cafe, Plant Centre, 360 degrees Multimedia Theatre, Conference Centre, Children's Activity Centre.
Disabled Access:	Yes. Toilets and parking for disabled on site. Wheelchair and motorised scooters on loan, booking necessary.
Tours/Events:	Daily guided tours. Full events programme.
Coach Parking:	Yes
Length of Visit:	4 hours
Booking Contact:	The National Botanic Garden of Wales, Llanarthne, Carmarthenshire, SA32 8HG. Telephone: 01558 668768 Fax: 01558 668933
Email:	info@gardenofwales.org.uk
Website:	www.gardenofwales.org.uk
Location:	About an hours drive from Cardiff, two hours drive from Bristol. Just off the A48, which links directly to the M4 and onto the M5.

Please quote this guide when booking

Clough Williams-Ellis inherited Plas Brondanw in 1908 and immediately set about creating the landscaped garden around his ancestral home just five miles from his more famous creation at Portmeirion. "It was for Brondanw's sake that I worked and stinted," wrote Sir Clough, "for its sake I chiefly hoped to prosper." The gardens at Plas Brondanw are considered by many to be of equal importance to his Italianate village at Portmeirion.

Brilliantly designed and conceived, it is a masterpiece of garden-making and one of the finest gardens inspired by the Arts and Crafts movement. Clough Williams-Ellis started with a beautiful site and fashioned a layout that confronts the lovely natural landscape, drawing its beauties into the heart of the garden. Several formal enclosures round the house are traversed by two main axes aligned on the pointed peak of Cnicht, as distinguished as any in Tuscany.

Fact File

Opening Times:	All Year
Admission Rates:	1st Adult £3.00 2nd & Subsequent Adult £2.00, Accompanied Children Free.
Group Rates:	Minimum group size: 10. By Appointment Only.
	Adult £2.00, All Children Free
Facilities:	None
Disabled Access:	Partial. Parking for disabled on site. Wheelchair on loan by appointment only.
	Toilet for disabled being upgraded in 2005. Please check with booking contact.
Tours/Events:	By arrangement
Coach Parking:	By appointment only
Length of Visit:	2 hours approx.
Booking Contact:	Lin Davies: 07880 766741, Davina Griffiths: Balfours, Windsor House, Windsor Place, Shrewsbury, SY1 2BZ. (01743 241181)
Email:	davinagriffiths@balfours-agents.net
Website:	www.virtualportmeirion.com
Location:	Signposted from A4058 on Croesor Road north of Llanfrothen Village.

Please quote this guide when booking

The Italianate village of Portmeirion is surrounded by 70 acres of sub-tropical woodlands known as *Y Gwyllt* ("the wild place"- it was once an area of rough pasture and gorse) with its Victorian shelters, temples and dogs' cemetery. From the 1840s successive tenants landscaped and planted the area with a variety of native and exotic trees. From the early 1900s the Gwyllt was developed by Caton Haig as an exotic woodland garden until his death in 1941 when the garden was bought by Clough Williams-Ellis and incorporated into his Portmeirion estate.

A tree trail has recently been established giving access to some of the most important trees in the garden including one hundred year old rhododendrons, gigantic Californian coast redwoods, the papauma or New Zealand 'dancing tree', the UK's largest Japanese cedar 'elegans' and tallest Chilean maiten tree, the ginkgo or maidenhair tree and many others.

Fact File

Opening Times:	All Year
Admission Rates:	Adult £6.00, Senior Citizen £5.00, Child £3.00
Group Rates:	Minimum group size: 12
	Adult £4.80, Senior Citizen £4.00, Child £2.40
Facilities:	Gift Shop, Plant Sales, Teas, Restaurant, Audio Visual, Hotel, 7 Shops, Tree Trail, Beach.
Disabled Access:	Yes. Toilet and parking for disabled on site. Wheelchair on loan, booking advisable.
Tours/Events:	None
Coach Parking:	Yes
Length of Visit:	3 hours
Booking Contact:	Terry Williams
	Portmerion, Gwynedd, LL48 6ET.
	Telephone: 01766 772311 Fax: 01766 771331
Email:	info@portmeirion-village.com
Website:	www.portmeirion-village.com
Location:	Signposted off A487 at Minffordd between Penrhyndeudraeth and Porthmadog.

Please quote this guide when booking

Rare Plant Fairs 2005

Rare plant fairs are a unique opportunity for all of us to get advice and ideas from experienced nurserymen and women who really know and care about plants. They can help us all choose plants that will thrive in our own gardens no matter where we live.

Rare plant fairs are held throughout England and Wales - many in beautiful locations which are a joy to visit. The range of plants on offer at the fairs covers just about everything you would wish for your garden from alpines and herbaceous perennials to trees, shrubs and tender sub-tropical plants for the sheltered garden or conservatory. Some plants will be new introductions to Britain, brought back by intrepid nurserymen and women from all over the globe.

It does not matter if you are a keen gardener with years of gardening experience, or a novice about to embark on your very first garden - a visit to one of the 2005 Rare Plant Fairs is a great day out for all.

Rare Plant Fairs Dates 2005

The Winter Gardens, Weston-Super-Mare	27th March 2005
Bath Pavilion, Bath	2nd April 2005
South West London	10th April 2005
Cheltenham Town Hall, Gloucestershire	16th April 2005
Quenington Old Rectory, Cirencester, Glouestershire	24th April 2005
Maxstoke Castle, Birmingham	1st May 2005
Caldicot Castle, South Wales	8th May 2005
Liscombe Park, Wing, Leighton Buzzard	15th May 2005
Oxford Botanic Arboretum	29th May 2005
Lackham College, Wiltshire	5th June 2005
Lullingstone Castle, Kent	12th June 2005
Westonbirt Arboretum, Gloucestershire	19th June 2005
Fonmon Castle, Nr Cardiff	26th June 2005
Englefield House, Reading	2nd July 2005
Lady Farm, Chelmwood, South Bath	10th July 2005
Sulgrave Manor, Banbury	16th July 2005
Harvington Hall, Kidderminster	21st August 2005
Abergavenny Castle, South Wales	27th August 2005

Fairs open between 11am and 4.30pm. Fairs cost between £3.50 and £4.00 *(No Concessions, children under 16 free with adult)*

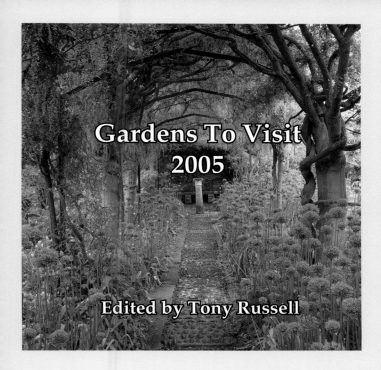

Gardens To Visit 2005

Edited by Tony Russell

"A fabulous publication...it looks fantastic".
The Royal Horticultural Society.

"Easy to use and informative".
Amateur Gardening Magazine.

"A wonderful book...just what
garden visitors are looking for".
Middleton Cheney Garden Club.

£8.95 plus £1.95 P&P

*'Gardens To Visit 2005' provides everything you need to
know when planning a garden visit.*

More than 160 of Britain's finest gardens depicted in all their glory.

The perfect gift for family and friends and the ideal companion for all your garden visits.

To order your copy of 'Gardens To Visit 2005' contact:

Publicity Works
P.O.Box 32
Tetbury
Gloucestershire
GL8 8BF

Telephone: 01453 836730
Fax: 01453 835285
Email: mail@publicity-works.org

Index

GARDENS TO VISIT 2005 is specially published for:

Publicity Works
P.O. Box 32
Tetbury
Gloucestershire
GL8 8BF
Telephone: 01453 836730 Fax: 01453 835285
Email: mail@publicity-works.org

IF YOU WOULD LIKE TO ORDER ADDITIONAL COPIES OF GARDENS TO VISIT 2005
PLEASE CONTACT THE ABOVE ADDRESS

Press and Media Specialists, Promotion, Publicity and Public Relations Consultants
and Event Organisers.

Thanks go to the Gardens and Garden Visitors who have provided feedback
on the information they would like to see within this publication.

ISBN 1 899803 23 8

Designed and Published by:

The WoodLand and Garden Publishing Company
Holmleigh Farm
Huntsgate
Gedney Broadgate
Spalding
Lincs PE12 0DJ

email: derekharris.associates@virgin.net